INTRODUCING PREHISTORY

The Lerner Archaeology Series
DIGGING UP THE PAST

INTRODUCING PREHISTORY

by Avraham Ronen

retold for young readers by Richard L. Currier

 Lerner Publications Company □ Minneapolis

Designed by Ofra Kamar

LIBRARY OF CONGRESS CATALOGING IN PUBLICATION DATA

Currier, Richard L.
Introducing prehistory.

(Digging up the Past: The Lerner Archaeology Series)
Includes index.
SUMMARY: Describes archaeological discoveries of prehistoric remains and the way in which these discoveries reveal human development in prehistoric times.

1. Man, Prehistoric—Juvenile literature. 2. Human evolution—Juvenile literature. [Man, Prehistoric. 2. Human evolution.] I. **Ronen, Avraham**, author. II. Title.

GN744.C87 1976   930'.1   72-10803
ISBN 0-8225-0833-8

This book is also cataloged under the name of Avraham Ronen.

This edition copyright © 1980 by Lerner Publications Company.
First published in the United States of America 1976 by Lerner Publications Company.

Original edition copyright © 1976 by G. A. The Jerusalem Publishing House Ltd.,
39 Tchernechovski Street, P.O. Box 7147, Jerusalem, Israel.

All rights reserved. International copyright secured. No part of this book may be reproduced in any form whatsoever without permission in writing from the publisher except for the inclusion of brief quotations in an acknowledged review.

International Standard Book Number: 0-8225-0833-8
Library of Congress Catalog Card Number: 72-10803

Manufactured in the United States of America
2 3 4 5 6 7 8 9 10 85 84 83 82 81 80

CONTENTS

PART I	WHAT IS PREHISTORY?	7
	1. The Great Span of Prehistoric Time	7
	2. Prehistorians and Other Archaeologists	8
PART II	THE PREHISTORIAN'S JOB	12
	1. Search, or Destroy?	15
	2. Analyzing Prehistoric Remains in the Laboratory	30
	3. How Old is "Old"?	30
PART III	MONKEYS, APES, AND HUMANS	39
	1. Tools, Chimps, and Logic	40
	2. Standing Erect	42
	3. Language and Learning	43
PART IV	THE FIRST HUMANS	46
	1. Ramapithecus	46
	2. Small-Brained Australopithecus and a Large-Brained Mystery	48
	3. Oldowan Tools	49
	4. What Were the First Humans Like?	53
PART V	THE REVOLUTIONARY HUNTERS AND FIRE BUILDERS	56
	1. Homo Erectus and the New Stone Tools	56
	2. The Mastery of Fire	60
PART VI	PEOPLE LIKE US	63
	1. Life After Death	63
	2. Cave Dwellers and Their Tools	66
	3. Modern People and Their Arts	73
	4. Precision in Stone Tools	75

PART VII	THE DAWN OF HISTORY	81
	1. The Ancient Grain Belt	83
	2. The Pursuit of Wealth	86
	3. The Dawn of History	86
GLOSSARY		91
INDEX		94

I WHAT IS PREHISTORY?

When people speak of "human history," they are usually referring to the actions and achievements of civilized human beings during the past 5,000 years or so. Much is known about this part of the history of our species because civilized people knew how to write, and they left behind written records of their hopes, fears, beliefs, and achievements.

Because the study of human history has depended so much on the study of written records, however, we have sometimes received an incorrect impression of just how long that history really is. We may think of our history as having begun in the fertile river valleys of the ancient Middle East, in the cities of the ancient Sumerians and Egyptians. Or perhaps we think of the temples and palaces of ancient China, or the pyramids of the Aztecs and the great walled cities of the Incas, whose civilizations flourished in the New World. But human history *really* began on the grassy plains of East Africa about 3 million years ago, among apelike creatures who stood erect and made crude stone tools but whom we almost hesitate to call "human."

The Great Span of Prehistoric Time

There is an old saying that "there is nothing new under the sun." Historians tell us that when they study the history of civilization since its earliest beginnings, they see the same patterns constantly repeating themselves: patterns of war, revolution, and conquest; growth, prosperity, decline, and depression; invention and destruction; birth and death. Seen through written records, history does indeed seem to repeat itself, and—except for technological advances—there really does seem to be nothing new under the sun.

But it is important to remember that the history of civilization goes back only about 5,000 years and that these years are only a tiny fraction of the 3-million-year period during which human beings have inhabited this planet. To get a better idea of the difference between these two spans of time, imagine that this book represents the entire 3 million years of human history, each page of the book representing an equal portion of that time span. As you turned the pages of the book, you would see the slowly evolving human species living in small bands as hunters and gatherers, moving their camps from place to place to follow the migrations of game animals and the seasonal appearance of wild fruits and vegetables. Although these wanderers would develop better weapons, dwellings, and other material objects, their basic way of life would be little changed throughout all but the last *page* of the book. About halfway down the last page, people would begin to settle down in permanent villages and to farm the land, growing their own food. Then in the last two or three sentences of the last page, the very first cities would appear, and with them, the beginnings of civilization and the invention of writing. It is this very last bit of human history, called "recorded history," that we know about in detail. You can see how it has given us a rather narrow view of the human experience of this planet!

For the brief time that civilization and recorded history have existed, many things have indeed remained the same. Thus, to understand how profoundly human life has changed since its beginnings, we must look at *all* of human history and read all those pages in our imaginary book of human life. Those pages represent more than 99 percent of the time that humans have inhabited the earth. They make up that vast span of human experience called "prehistory."

As you will see, the changes in human life since its beginnings have been profound indeed. The human body has changed and grown in certain ways, the human brain has expanded to twice its original size, and the very nature of human life has changed enormously. In the beginning, humans had an existence similar to that of other animals. By the end of prehistoric times, however, humans had developed a way of life that no other living thing on our planet had ever achieved or experienced.

Prehistorians and Other Archaeologists

Scientists who study the remains of very ancient people are called "archaeologists." Their job is to locate and recover ancient cities, houses, graves, tools, and other ancient remains, whether they are buried in desert sands, locked up in ancient pyramids and tombs, or lying on the bottom of the ocean. "Prehistorians" are a special group of archaeologists who study only the remains of prehistoric people, and they must cope with some special problems that most other archaeologists do not face.

Other archaeologists, for example, are primarily concerned with the remains of civilized people, who live either in cities or in permanent villages. The civilized people of ancient times left behind in such settlements large accumulations of graves, workshops, public buildings, temples, and the discarded objects of everyday life. A city or village might be inhabited for hundreds or even thousands of years by a fairly large number of people, and in this way many tons of material would come eventually to be deposited all in one place. Sooner or later, a war, an outbreak of disease, a famine, or a ruinous fire might drive the people from their homes, and they might abandon the village or the city. Such a large pile of material will have been accumulated by that time, however, that it will not be especially difficult for archaeologists to locate the ancient site. When they dig down into it, they are likely to find large quantities of ancient objects.

The prehistorian, on the other hand, deals with human groups that wandered about, hunting and gathering wild foods to supply their daily needs. These people rarely stayed in one place for very long, and therefore they seldom left behind more than a few bits and pieces of cast-off materials. Thus the prehistorian, to be successful in his quest for remains from the past, must be a good detective. He must try to guess where human beings who lived thousands —or even millions—of years ago would have camped, where they might have slept at night, where they might have made a large kill of game animals, and where they might have set up their temporary workshops to make stone tools.

Prehistoric archaeology presents quite a challenge, for there are some very serious difficulties that must be overcome before the secrets of prehistoric times can be revealed. First of all, the search for evidence of prehistoric life has only just begun. Archaeologists have been searching for prehistoric remains for only about 150 years, and much ground still remains to be covered. Entire areas of the world have hardly begun to be investigated, and other areas have not been investigated at all. In fact, most prehistoric archaeologists have carried out their investigations in just a few parts of the world, mainly in Europe, North America, and East Africa. Most of Africa, Asia, South America, and Australia are still almost unexplored territory.

Second, prehistoric people left behind no written records, and we can only guess what languages they spoke, what kinds of poems and stories they told, what kinds of tribal laws and customs they lived by, and what gods and spirits they believed in. Finally, most of the objects used by prehistoric people were made of wood, leather, fiber, bone, hair, and other perishable materials. We call these materials "perishable" because they almost never last more than a few hundred years after they are discarded. And since prehistoric people lived tens of thousands or even hundreds of thousands of years ago, almost all of the objects they made and used have long since rotted away and returned to the soil. Stone is one of the few nonperishable materials used in prehistoric times, and stone tools are thus one of the trademarks of prehistoric peoples.

If prehistoric people had made their tools and weapons out of metal, we would know even less about them today, for metal gradually corrodes and disappears into the soil. But stones can lie buried in the soil almost indefinitely without changing in any significant way. Since each small prehistoric tribe or band made stone tools by the thousands, it is mostly through these tools that we have come to know about the lives and activities of prehistoric humans. This is why we will be talking about stone tools throughout most of this book. You may be surprised to learn how much stone tools can tell us about the lives of human beings who lived thousands of years before the beginning of civilization.

The small amounts of evidence that prehistorians must rely on (and the absence of so much information that we would like to have) mean that much of what we will say about prehistoric people is really guesswork. These are not just ordinary guesses, however; they are the best guesses that many trained scientists have made on the basis of most of the evidence in existence now. As more parts of the world are explored, and as more is learned about prehistoric people in general, scientists will probably realize that some of these guesses were wrong.

Thus it is important that we be cautious about much of this information and not assume that *everything* scientists now believe is the final truth. Because there is still so much to learn and because our knowledge of prehistoric life is so new that scientists have not had many years to study it, the most basic conclusions of prehistoric archaeologists are constantly changing. This was once as common in the fields of physics, chemistry, biology, and medicine as it is in prehistory today. Such change and confusion—typical of new and growing fields of science—offer us the rare opportunity to follow at close hand the development of a whole new realm of human knowledge and understanding.

Most of this book is devoted to describing the lives of our prehistoric ancestors, the kinds of problems that they faced, the kinds of tools and houses that they constructed, and the discoveries and inventions that they made and passed on to future generations. But before we begin the fascinating story of prehistory, we would first like to tell you about the scientists who study prehistoric people, and about the methods they use to find, preserve, and understand the rare and often mysterious scraps of material that are all that is left of prehistoric life.

II THE PREHISTORIAN'S JOB

Most of the objects from prehistoric times that archaeologists find are buried in the ground, but once in a while some prehistoric object is found just lying on the surface in plain sight. Unfortunately, such objects are usually badly damaged because they have been exposed to the weather for a long time. Thus their scientific value has been virtually destroyed. But such surface finds are important in a different way: they usually indicate that there are many more prehistoric objects nearby, buried in the ground out of sight.

When an archaeologist finds a prehistoric object on the surface, he or she will carefully mark the spot where it was found. The archaeologists can then return at some later time, bringing special digging tools and other people to help, and the entire area can be explored. A place where a group of prehistoric objects has been found—or even a single object, if it is important enough—is called a "prehistoric site." Most of the prehistoric sites that we know of were found when someone noticed an object on the surface and then dug beneath the surface to search for more.

Although prehistoric people are often thought of as cave dwellers, only a small fraction of them really did live in caves. Most prehistoric people lived in the open, building simple shelters that they abandoned after a few weeks when the wandering band moved on to the next location. Thus while some prehistoric sites are found in caves, many more are found in the open, often near a lake or a river or on the edge of a forest. If a site provided an abundance of wild foods, a nearby source of water, and natural protection from enemies, prehistoric people probably made camp there at some time.

When archaeologists locate a prehistoric site, they do not just take a pick and shovel and dig up everything in the area. Instead, the soil is

THE PREHISTORIAN'S JOB

This cave, discovered at Mount Carmel in Israel, was inhabited by humans in prehistoric times.

removed very slowly and carefully according to special techniques. This process of removing the soil and recovering buried objects from a site is called "excavation." Archaeological excavation is a difficult, delicate, time-consuming, and costly operation, often requiring the combined efforts of a whole team of experts and workers.

After the remains have been excavated (and, in many cases, specially treated to insure that they will be properly preserved), they are taken to archaeological laboratories and museums where they can be studied more carefully. Eventually, the archaeologists will write a report —or perhaps a whole series of reports—about the remains they found and excavated. These reports are published in scientific journals and read by hundreds of other archaeologists all over the world, who compare the new information with the results of their own work. In this way, all archaeologists work together to build a clearer and more correct picture of what human beings were doing in the distant past.

Every prehistoric site contains two different types of remains that are of interest to the archaeologist. The first type consists of things that are directly connected with the human beings who once lived there. These include remains of the human body, such as bones, skulls, or teeth; small hand-made objects such as tools, weapons, and objects of religious or artistic value; and traces of human dwellings, such as the remains of walls, fireplaces, storage pits, or smooth dirt floors.

The other type of archaeological remains consists of things that provide information about the ancient environment of a particular site. Such remains would not be important if the environment remained the same as time passes. But the earth's environments are constantly changing, although the changes are usually occurring too slowly to be noticed within a single lifetime. With the passage of thousands or millions of years, however, regions that were once covered with forests may gradually turn into grasslands, marshes may dry out and turn into deserts, large areas of the earth's surface may become submerged beneath the sea, and other regions once submerged may become dry land.

There have been periods in the past when the earth has grown cold, and the great sheets of ice at the polar regions have grown larger and larger, spilling down over the warmer lands toward the equator and crushing everything in their path. At other times, the earth has grown much warmer than it is today, and vast areas of land have turned into steamy, swampy jungles. Tall mountain ranges have gradually eroded away and subsided into gently rounded hills; in other regions, flat land has been pushed upward by forces deep inside the earth to become jagged new mountain ranges.

The result of all this activity is that the earth's many environments are constantly changing. Since new forms of plant and animal life are also constantly appearing through evolution, the environment of any one spot on the earth's surface rarely remains the same for very long. After a few thousand years have passed, significant changes in the environment are almost certain to have taken place. Thus, we cannot know exactly what the environment at a particular site was like thousands of years ago simply by studying the environment that exists there today. But by digging up the remains of plants and animals found deep in the soil, archaeologists and other scientists can often tell much about the prehistoric environment.

The remains of animal bones, for example, show what kinds of animals inhabited that region in past times. Sometimes it is possible to tell, from the way certain bones have been broken or smashed, which animals were actually eaten by the prehistoric humans who once lived there. Plant remains, too, can be identified, especially the seeds and pollen grains that may be found in the soil even after thousands of years. Many of the methods that archaeologists use to find and analyze the plant and animal remains of prehistoric times are very new; they have only been used for the last 15 or 20 years.

Search, or Destroy?

When archaeologists begin the work of excavating an archaeological site, they assume one of the heaviest burdens of responsibility faced by any modern scientist. In order to carry out their search for ancient objects, they must destroy the site that contains the remains of these objects.

Modern methods of archaeology insure that no object, however small, will be overlooked. As the soil is removed from the site, it is broken up and passed through strainers, in order to catch small objects like coins, beads, teeth, and even sewing needles that may have survived intact. All objects of interest are re-

THE PREHISTORIAN'S JOB

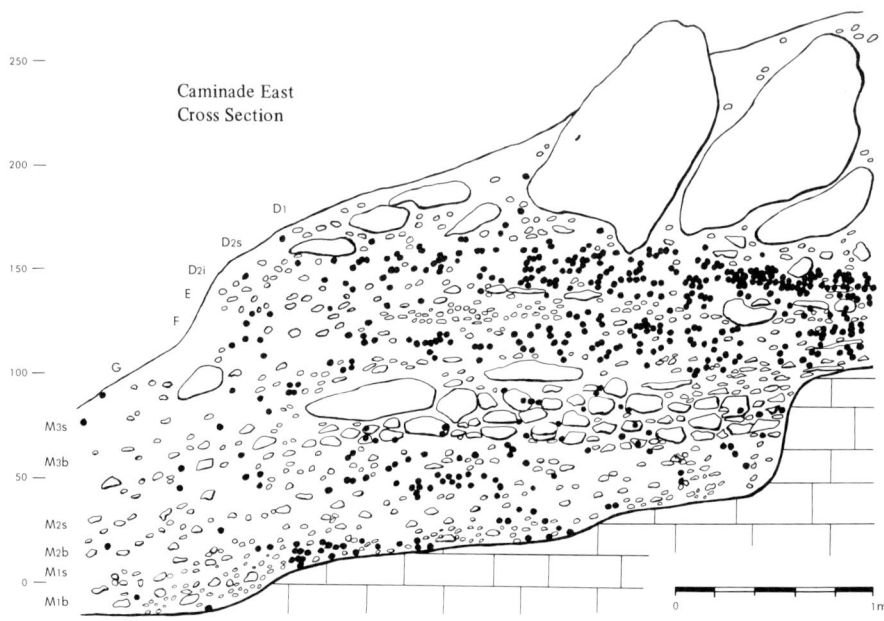

A cross-section drawing of a prehistoric site in France, showing the different archaeological levels. The black dots indicate the location of stone implements.

moved and set aside, and the leftover soil, sand, gravel, and rock is simply piled in a heap. Thus, once a site has been dug up, it has been destroyed forever. To try and put a site back together after it has been excavated would be somewhat like trying to put a tree back together after it has been sawed into lumber.

Since archaeologists know that they are destroying each site as they excavate it, they are extremely careful to keep complete records of everything they see and find as the work progresses. Numerous photographs are taken of the site at different stages of excavation, maps and charts are made showing the different types of soil at different levels, and the exact location and position of each object are carefully noted before it is removed.

These methods insure that it will be possible to go back and check the records if, in the future, archaeologists need to have information about

THE PREHISTORIAN'S JOB

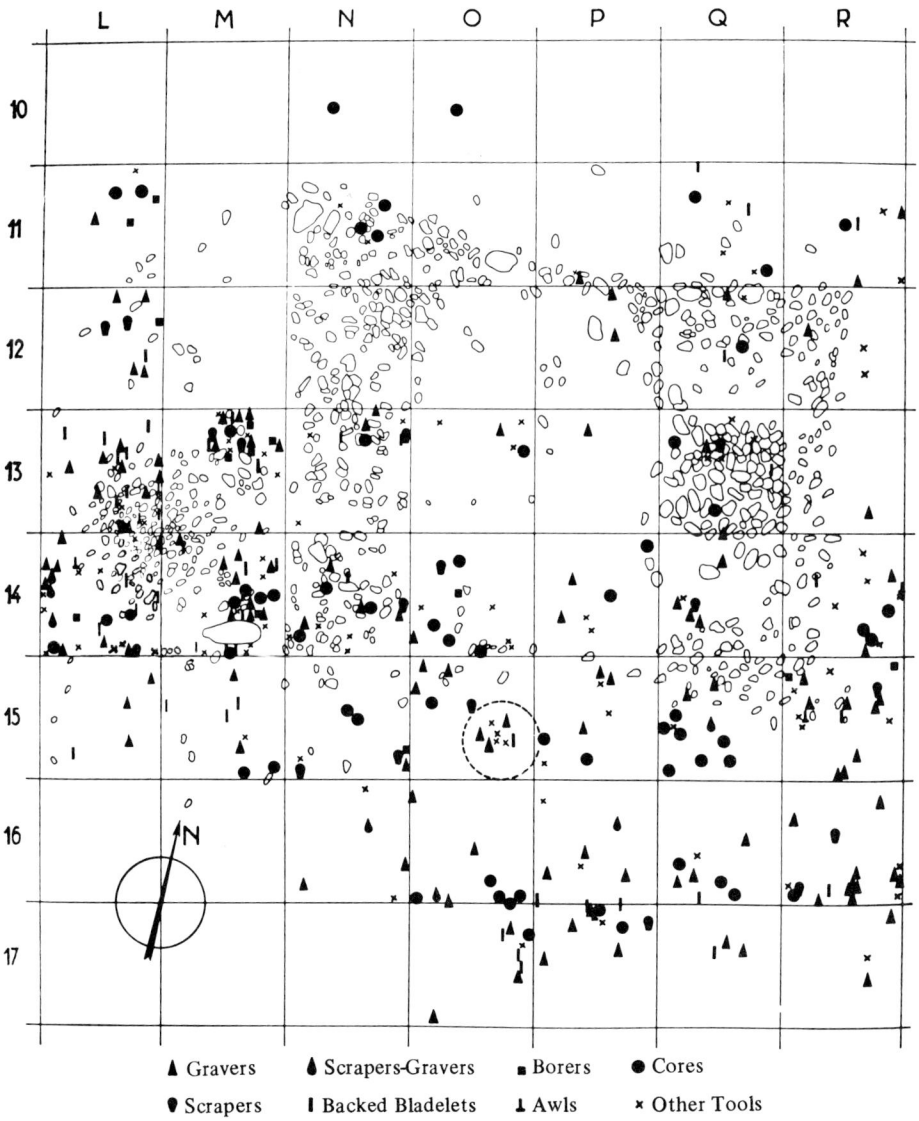

▲ Gravers   ◖ Scrapers-Gravers   ■ Borers   ● Cores
◉ Scrapers   I Backed Bladelets   ⊥ Awls   × Other Tools

Archaeologists drew this map to record the positions of stone tools and heaps of pebbles found at a prehistoric site.

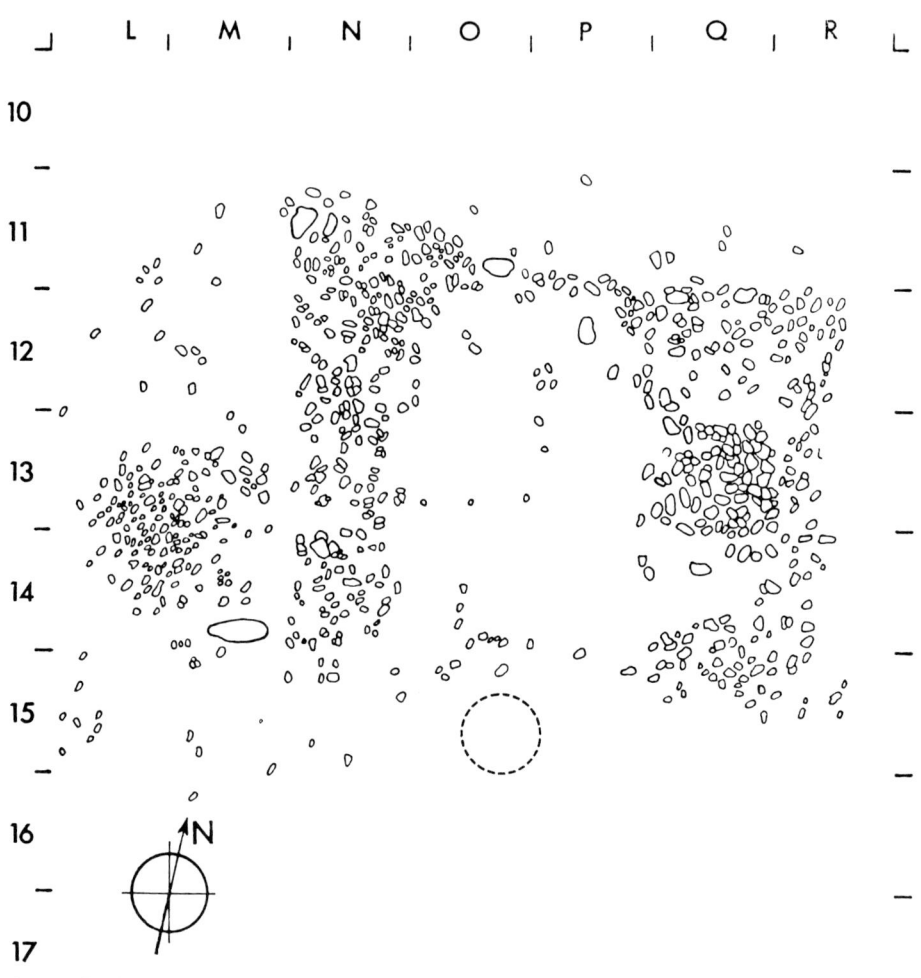

Above and right: On closer examination, the archaeologists discovered that the shapeless heaps of pebbles were actually the remains of a prehistoric dwelling.

the site that may not have seemed important at the time it was excavated. For example, archaeologists excavating a site might remove stones of irregular shape that do not seem to have any special meaning or importance. Even so, they will record the exact position of each stone as it is removed. Later, when the positions of all the stones are drawn on

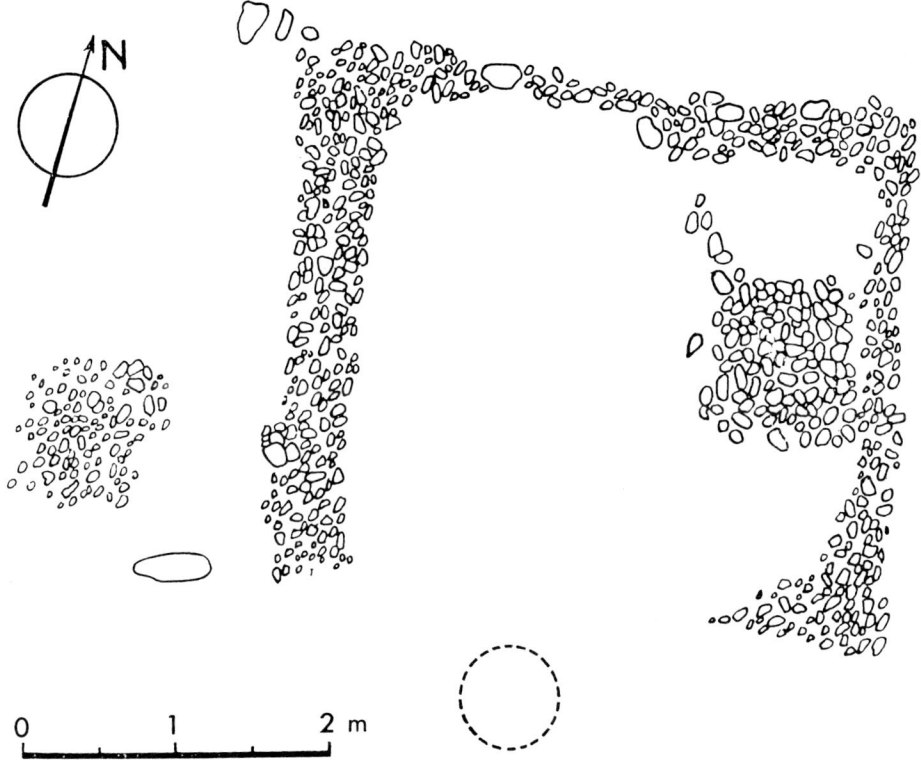

a map, it may suddenly become obvious that some of the stones were buried in a straight line or in a circle. Such a discovery would indicate that the stones might have been part of a wall or a fireplace that was overlooked during the actual process of excavation.

All archaeologists follow these methods, but prehistoric archaeologists are the most careful and meticulous of all. The objects they are looking for are much smaller and more difficult to find than the tombs, temples, cities, and pyramids that other archaeologists—who study the remains of civilized societies—may be looking for. After sifting all the excavated soil through a strainer, the prehistoric archaeologist even mixes it with water, in case the remains of any insects, seeds, or even microorganisms are still present in the soil after thousands of years.

THE PREHISTORIAN'S JOB

EXCAVATING A PREHISTORIC SITE

The pictures on pages 20 through 29 show the various stages in an excavation conducted by the author at Hefziba, Israel.

Stone tools lying on the surface of the ground alert archaeologists to the existence of a prehistoric site.

THE PREHISTORIAN'S JOB

The surface finds are collected after a grid of ropes is placed over the site. This grid enables archaeologists to mark the exact location of each find.

THE PREHISTORIAN'S JOB 22

A trench is dug at the site in order to locate implements buried in the ground.

THE PREHISTORIAN'S JOB

Workers use brushes to clear away dirt in the trench. Each find that they make is carefully recorded in a notebook.

THE PREHISTORIAN'S JOB

As work continues on the trench, an archaeological layer containing stone implements and bone fragments is revealed. The pieces of bone are the discarded remains of the meals of ancient hunters.

Archaeologists find a "living-floor" on which prehistoric people actually walked. The stone implements scattered on the floor are about 15,000 years old.

THE PREHISTORIAN'S JOB 26

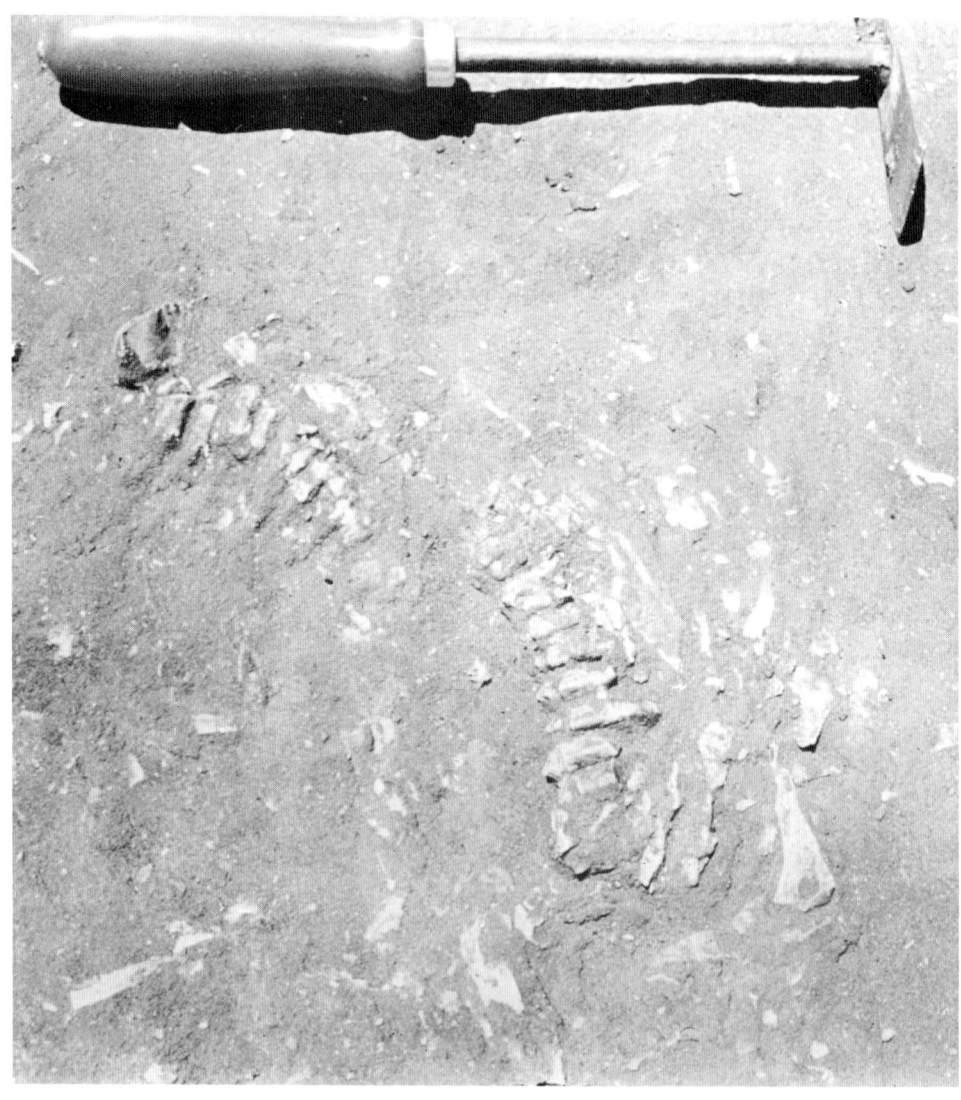

In another area of the same living-floor, the jaw bones and the teeth of deer are discovered. This find indicates that the prehistoric people who lived on the site hunted and ate deer.

The discovery of the teeth of wild cattle suggests to the archaeologists that these animals were also a prey of the prehistoric hunters.

THE PREHISTORIAN'S JOB

Another important find is this large fragment of a 15,000-year-old mortar, a vessel used in grinding materials such as grains. The archaeologists had not expected to find such an ancient implement of this type.

The first trench at Hefziba is completed, and the archaeological layer in it has been excavated. But there is much more work to be done at the site, and much more to be learned about the people who inhabited it. The excavation will continue.

Analyzing Prehistoric Remains in the Laboratory

After prehistoric remains have been found and removed from the archaeological site, they are often taken to the laboratory to be analyzed. There, chemical tests, microscopic examination, and other scientific techniques often provide information about the objects themselves that cannot be gained by observation alone.

The remains of ancient fireplaces are analyzed to determine what kinds of materials were burned in them. Wood, fat and oils, and manure—all of which are used by prehistoric people as fuel—leave certain kinds of residues that can be identified by laboratory analysis. It is even possible, through the analysis of the stones lining the fireplace, to determine how hot the fire was. This may be important, since fires that are used for cooking need to be much hotter than fires used for warmth and light. Finally, the charred pieces of wood or bone that an ancient fireplace may contain are extremely valuable finds to the prehistorian. Such remains can often be analyzed for the radioactive carbon they contain. This kind of analysis makes it possible to determine approximately when the site was occupied.

The bones of animals found at the site are counted and examined, and from this information it is often possible to tell not only what prehistoric people were eating for dinner but even how much meat they ate—and which kinds of animals this meat came from. When this information is combined with the analysis of seeds and pollen grains, archaeologists can reconstruct a reasonably accurate picture of the environment of that particular place at a particular time in the past. Piece by piece, the great puzzle is slowly put together.

How Old is "Old"?

Of all the questions that the archaeologist must find answers to, the question of age is probably the most important of all. Knowing the age of an object will help the archaeologist to determine not only how long the object has been buried in the ground but also who used it, where it came from, and even what its purpose may have been. The question of age is vitally important, but it is also very difficult to answer. The products of civilized societies often bear the names or images of known historical rulers or may even—in the case of written records and coins—have the date written or stamped directly on them, but the objects left behind by prehistoric people contain no clear indication of their age. Thus the prehistoric archaeologist must rely on other kinds of information to determine when an object was made, when it was lost or thrown away, and when it came to be buried in the place where it was found.

The most common method of dating is based on the principle called "stratigraphy." When people live in a certain place over a period of time, the things they discard—as well as the mud and dust from their feet—gradually build up a layer, or *stratum,* of material. This layer may be anywhere from a few inches to several feet thick, depending on how fast it accumulated and how long the people continued to live on the site. Eventually, however, a time will come when, for some reason, the site will be abandoned, and wild plants and animals will take over. The wildlife will also deposit material, but this material will look and feel different from the human deposits.

After time passes, a different group of people may move into the region and choose the same site for their own living quarters. (This happens quite commonly, because the same natural features that attracted the first inhabitants may also attract settlers in a later age.) The new inhabitants have their own particular style of life; they use different tools and weapons, eat different foods, and throw out different kinds of garbage. Thus they will add another layer of material, different both from that of the original settlers and from that of the wild plants and animals who had taken over.

This imaginary site will now have at least four different layers, or *strata.* First, there is the stratum originally formed by the wildlife of the region. Second, there is the stratum of the earliest human settlement. Third, there is the stratum formed by wildlife when the original settlers abandoned the site, and fourth, there is the stratum formed by the new inhabitants.

Since each new stratum is laid down on top of the previous one, the strata on top are always newer than the strata on the bottom. Thus, when an archaeologist digs down into an archaeological site, the upper strata are always assumed to be the youngest, while the lower strata are assumed to be the oldest.

Stratigraphy can usually tell us which objects in a site are older and which are younger, according to the depth of the stratum in which they are found. But stratigraphy cannot tell us how old an object is. For this, archaeologists must use other methods, the most important of which is called "carbon-14 dating."

Carbon-14 dating is made possible by the fact that the radioactive isotope carbon 14 steadily changes by itself into ordinary carbon 12, and it changes at a certain, fixed speed. Since all organisms absorb carbon 14 from the environment while they are alive, they all have about the same percentage of it in their bodies when they die. After death, however, the percentage of carbon 14 begins to decrease.

After 5,600 years, half of the carbon 14 has disappeared, having changed into ordinary carbon. After another 5,600 years, half of the remainder will have disappeared, and so on. This gradual change makes it possible for scientists to determine the approximate age of a piece of wood, bone, leather, fiber, or other dead organic material simply by measuring the radioactive carbon it contains. If it has about half as much carbon 14 as a living organism, then it is about 5,600 years old. If it has only one-quarter as much, then it is about 11,200 years old. If it has only one-eighth as much, then it is about 16,800 years old, and so on.

After the material is about 50,000 years old, however, the amount of radioactive carbon still left is so small that it cannot be accurately measured, and carbon-14 dating can no longer be used. There are, however, other radioactive elements that change even more slowly. The most useful of these is the radioactive form of potassium, called "potassium 40." This element changes into the gas called "argon" so slowly that scientists can use it to measure the age of certain volcanic rocks that were formed millions of years ago.

Right: Flint blades and the cores from which they were struck

Overleaf left: A carving of a woman's head, found at Bressempuy, France

Overleaf right: A 25,000-year-old Venus figurine carved in a block of limestone, from Laussel, France. (See page 75 for more information about such figurines.)

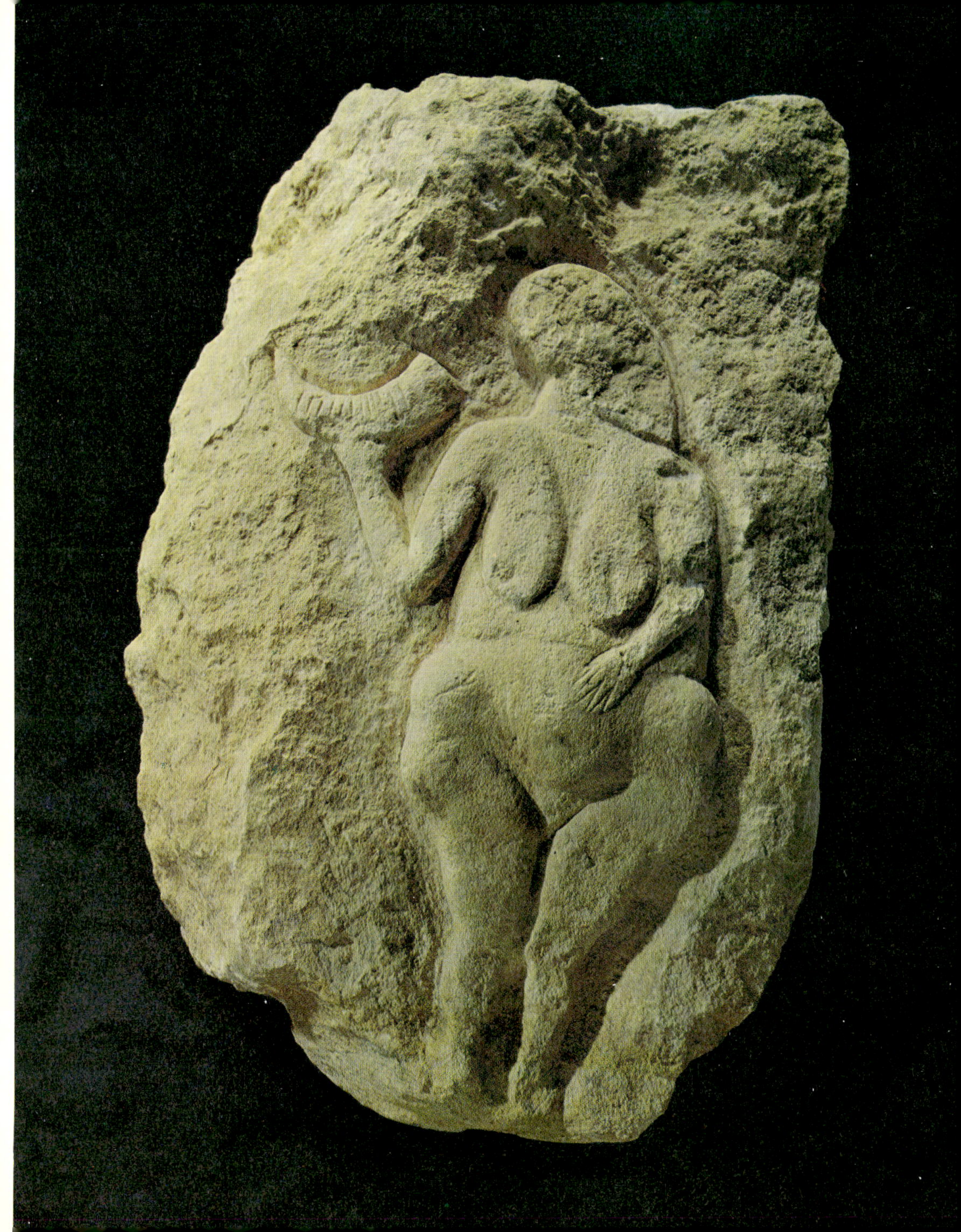

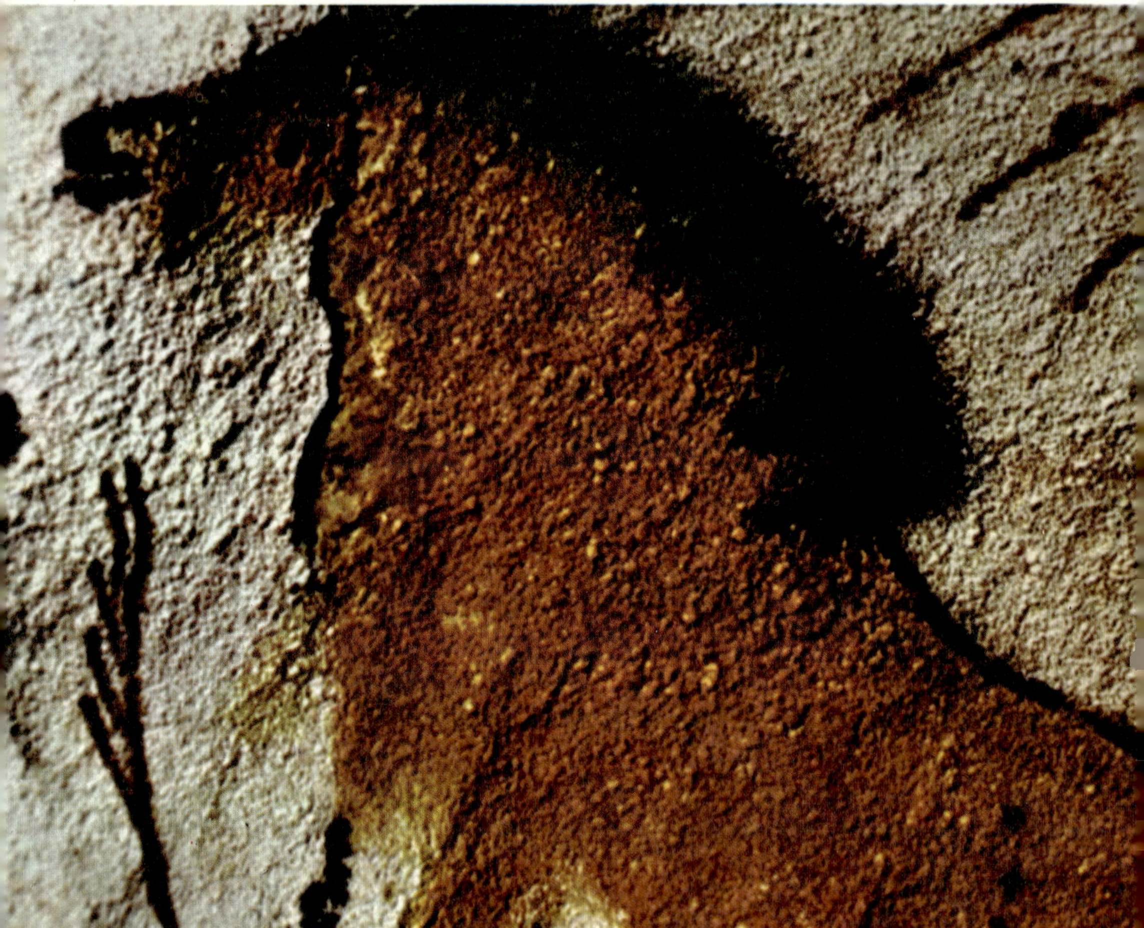

Thus, if the age of some dead organic material is less than 50,000 years, the carbon-14 method can be used to determine its age fairly accurately. If the remains in a site are much older, the potassium-argon method can sometimes be used to determine the age of the surrounding rocks. With these two methods, the entire history of human life on earth can be covered.

In the case of carbon-14 dating, the charred wood and pieces of bone often found in ancient fireplaces can be very useful. When an object has been charred and blackened by fire, it is no longer as likely to rot and disappear into the soil, yet most of the carbon still remains. (Carbon, in fact, is what gives the object its blackened appearance.) Scientists can use the carbon to find a carbon-14 date and thus determine the moment in history when the ancient fire was made.

The main problem with carbon-14 dating is that it depends on the archaeologist's ability to find organic material in the site. Organic material is the remains of living organisms, either plant or animal; only this once-living material can be dated by the carbon-14 method. The longer an organic object like a bone, a skull, a spear, or a rope remains in the soil, the more likely it is to rot and disappear entirely. Thus, although there is a fair amount of organic material still left in sites that are two or three thousand years old, there is little organic material left in sites that are tens of thousands of years old. At the same time, the potassium-argon method is even more limited, for only a few prehistoric sites contain the right kinds of volcanic rocks that can be dated with this method.

These are, however, only some of the methods archaeologists use to study the remains of prehistoric people. There are many other new methods available, and still more will probably be developed in the future to make the archaeologist's task easier. But not even the fanciest and most complicated scientific techniques can, by themselves, make sense out of the strange and unfamiliar objects that prehistorians remove from the earth.

It is one thing to find the remains of prehistoric objects, but it is quite another thing to figure out how they were used, how they were made, or what they can tell us about the lives of prehistoric human beings. For this kind of analysis, it is important to know how people live in tribal societies and how our close relatives

Left: The image of a horse painted on the wall of a cave at Lascaux, France. This ancient painting is about 15,000 years old.

in the animal kingdom—the monkeys and apes—live in their natural habitats.

Although there is much that we do not yet understand about the beginning of human life, we do know that the first human beings were, in many ways, partly like apes and partly like ourselves. In the next chapter, we will talk about some of the information that can help us make good guesses about what human life was like two or three million years ago.

III MONKEYS, APES, AND HUMANS

According to the Bible, the human race was created "to replenish the earth, and subdue it: and have dominion...over every living thing that moveth upon the earth." For centuries, people accepted this concept without question. The idea that God intended the human race to subdue and control the natural world fit in well with the belief that humans had been created separately from all other living things. But some revolutionary developments in science that occurred during the 19th century cast doubt on these traditional ideas about where our species came from and what its proper purpose on this planet might be. Two events, in particular, illustrate the important new direction in which science was moving at that time.

In 1856, the remains of a strange skeleton were found in the Neanderthal Valley in Germany. Clearly the bones did not come from any known ape, monkey, or other living species of animal, because the skeleton — especially the skull — was almost the same as that of a human. Yet at the same time it was different from any human skeleton anyone had ever seen. In time, scientists concluded that the skeleton had belonged to a human, but nevertheless a human very different from people like us. Eventually, this type of human being came to be called "Neanderthal Man." Since the discovery of those first Neanderthal remains, many other skulls and bones of Neanderthal men, women, and children have been found.

The second important event occurred just three years later, in 1859, when Charles Darwin published his famous and important book entitled *On the Origin of Species by Means of Natural Selection or the Preservation of Favored Races in the Struggle for Life*. In this book, Darwin proposed his theory of evolution, explaining how many animal species gradually change with the passage of time, eventually giving rise to new species that have never existed before. People argued bitterly about Darwin's theories for years afterwards, but most people in the modern world eventually came to accept the idea of evolution.

It is not difficult to see how these two events of the 19th century changed our ways of thinking about humanity. If plants and animals had not been suddenly created by God but had gradually evolved from other species, then human beings must also have evolved from other animal species. The Neanderthal skeleton — as well as other prehistoric skeletons that were found later — showed that a type of human no longer in existence had once lived on the earth. Today, most people have come to believe that our own kind evolved from the Neanderthals and they themselves evolved from still other types of prehistoric humans.

While we humans may have evolved from other animals, it is clear that we are more than just another animal species. We have accomplished things that no other animals have accomplished, from building fires to landing on the moon. What is so different about our minds and bodies that has enabled us to do things that no other form of life even dreamed of doing before?

Tools, Chimps, and Logic

Before we try to answer this question, let us take a look at some of the things that we humans have in common with other animals. It may surprise you to learn that human beings are not the only animals who make tools, communicate with each other, teach their young how to behave, or use logic in solving problems. At one time, scientists believed that only humans could do such things, but careful study of the behavior of apes and monkeys in the wild has revealed that some of our nearest relatives in the animal kingdom can do them too.

Animals were once believed to act only according to instinct, and humans were considered to act only according to logic and learning. But we now know that while the simpler animals, such as insects or worms, may live purely by following their instincts, the more complex animals, such as dogs, porpoises, monkeys, and apes, have to learn even such basic things as what kinds of foods to eat and how to greet each other. Chimpanzees, for example, learn different forms of greeting. Some chimpanzees exchange greetings by touching each other's hips, while other chimps greet each other by touching hands. (Does this sound familiar?) When two groups of chimpanzees meet in the forest, they often have a noisy "festivity" that sounds to human ears very much like a boisterous party.

Perhaps most surprising of all was the discovery, made only a few years ago by the famous British scientist Jane Goodall, that wild chimpanzees make tools. Until Jane Goodall announced the results of her research, tool-making was considered one of the most basic differences between humans and other animals.

The chimpanzee's tool-making is inspired by the animal's appetite for termites. It seems that while chimpanzees love to eat termites, the termite nests of Africa are as hard as concrete, and the chimps cannot break them open to get at the tiny insects inside. But there are small openings that the termites use to enter and leave their nests, and it is through these tiny holes that the chimps have learned to capture their prey. To do this, a chimpanzee first selects a thin twig from a tree, strips the leaves off it, and breaks it to the correct length. He carries this termite stick to the location of the termite nest and pushes it into the entrance. The termites swarm onto the stick, and the chimp then pulls the stick out and happily licks the termites off.

The reason scientists call this termite stick a "tool"—and consider it so important—is that the chimpanzee must perform many different actions before ever getting to the termites he wants to eat. This shows that chimps can work intelligently toward a goal and that they can make plans. A chimp can form the *idea* of eating the termites while he is still up in the tree breaking off the twig, even if the termite nest is not in sight. Mental capacities such as these are rare among animals, however. The baboon, a large and intelligent monkey, has never learned to make termite sticks, even though baboons have watched the chimps doing this, and they too are fond of termites.

For a long time, scientists thought that the non-vegetable foods in monkey and ape diets consisted of small animals that were there for the taking, such as insects like termites, snails, or birds' eggs. But field studies have recently shown that some apes—and here again chimpanzees are the star performers—actually hunt and eat other animals. Even more important, they cooperate with each other in hunting wild game, and they share the meat if the hunt is successful. Cooperation and food-sharing—also considered "basic human activities"—were once believed to be unknown among apes and monkeys.

Another characteristic often considered peculiarly human is the prohibition of incest, or sexual intercourse between members of the same family. All human societies forbid incest, yet cats and dogs, horses and sheep, and most other animals do not seem to mind mating with their parents. This too was long considered one of the important differences between humans and other animals. But recent studies of the Japanese macaque (a medium-sized monkey) showed that, although male macaques will mate with almost any female in their group, they will not mate with their mothers.

An aversion to incest, a capacity for learning and for tool-making — these are some of the characteristics that humans seem to share with other animals. Of course, there is an enormous difference between a spacecraft or a computer on the one hand and a termite stick on the other. Though other animals can do many of the same kinds of things we do, there is much that they cannot do, and in most cases, the differences in abilities are greater than the similarities. But it is important to be aware of the similarities too, because they help us to understand how our human capabilities evolved from similar abilities in other animals.

Standing Erect

When our ape-like ancestors adopted a fully erect posture and began to travel entirely on their hind legs, they started on the evolutionary road that eventually led to people like us. These very first humans had small brains, and they probably looked more like apes than like people. But they were the first animals to have a strong and capable pair of limbs that were not needed for moving about.

As the first humans developed, their hind legs became long and slender, in contrast to the short, stubby hind legs of most apes and monkeys. These streamlined limbs were well suited for running and walking long distances. At that point, the forelimbs, which we call "arms," were free to be used for any purpose. The first humans quickly learned to use their arms and hands for throwing weapons, for making things, and for carrying things about. Since even these first humans lacked the powerful teeth and claws of their ape-like ancestors, they had no natural weapons with which to defend themselves. Thus it became even more important to fashion tools and weapons out of wood and stone.

In this way, erect posture, the freeing of the hands and arms for making and carrying things, and the loss of strong teeth and claws all worked together to create a new kind of approach to the problem of survival. While other animals might survive because they were strong and fast, humans tended to survive because they could make things with their hands. And making things requires intelligence and the ability to plan ahead.

In this new human way of life, it was the intelligent individual who survived and who lived to raise intelligent offspring. Gradually, the human brain began growing larger and larger, until it had more than doubled in size. Such an increase in intelligence made possible the development of a way of life based mainly on learning rather than on instinct. This system of *learning* how to live is what we call "culture."

Culture makes it possible for different groups of humans, living in different environments, to learn the special ways of life that enable them to survive, whether they live in jungles or great cities, on prairies or islands. Through the use of language, the adult members of the society can share their experiences, figure out how to cooperate with each other, and teach their offspring the culture of the group. In this way, language, learning, and culture are all connected, forming a distinctively *human* way of life not shared by any other animals.

Language and Learning

Monkeys and apes have vocal cords like ours, and their lips and tongues are flexible enough to form words. The chimpanzee, which is like us in so many other ways, has vocal organs so nearly identical to our own that scientists are convinced there is no physical reason why a chimp could not speak English—or any other language—with perfect pronunciation. Yet apes and monkeys cannot speak, because they lack the necessary brain power.

Our brains are constructed in a way that enables us to form *ideas* about things that are not actually happening at the time we are thinking about them. We can imagine what it might be like to do something in the future, in a different time and place. We can also imagine certain qualities of things without necessarily imagining the things themselves. For example, we do not have to imagine a red object or a loud sound to form the ideas of redness or loudness.

MONKEYS, APES, AND HUMANS

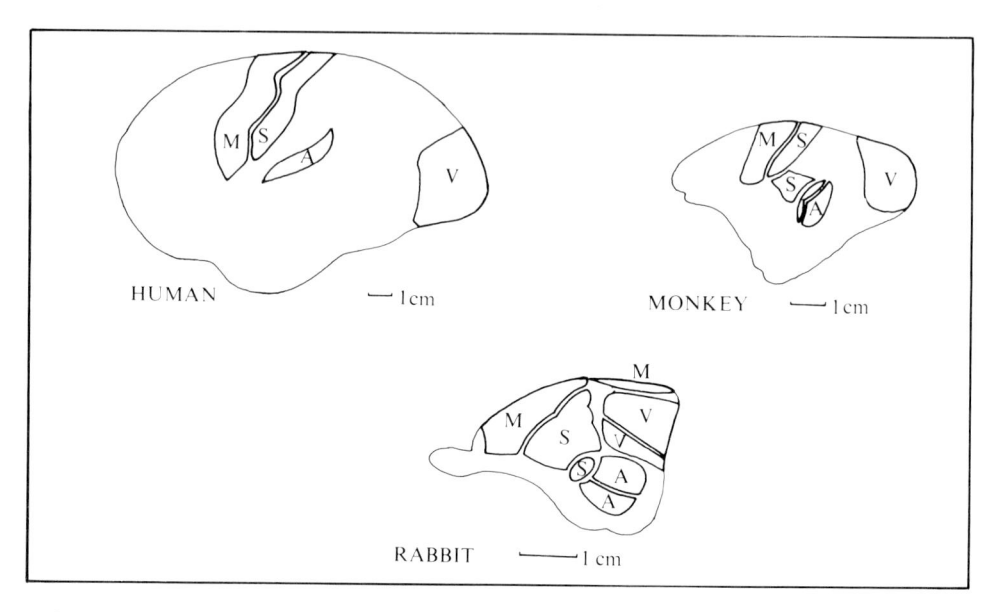

A drawing of the brains of a human, a monkey, and a rabbit showing the sensorimotor system, which receives nerve messages from the body and controls movement. The parts of this system are: A—auditory (hearing); M—motor (movement); S—somatic (sensation); V—visual. As you can see, only a small part of the human brain is involved in these basic functions. The largest part of the brain is free to deal with complex mental processes such as memory, speech, and thought.

As children, we learn to think in these ways by learning words that represent thoughts and ideas. We also learn to use these words to communicate thoughts and ideas to other people. No other animal is able to use sounds as we do to represent such abstract things. For example, chimpanzee babies who are brought up in human households never learn to speak. Their brains are simply not capable of doing the job.

We humans mature more slowly than almost any other animal. In the 15 or 20 years it takes us to reach adulthood, dogs, cats, goats, sheep, cows, pigs, monkeys, and many other animals live out their natural lives and die of old age. During the long years of childhood, our brains grow larger and larger. The brains of a human infant and a chimpanzee infant are about the same size at birth, but while the chimp's brain will increase about 25 percent as the animal grows up, the human's brain will increase about 400 percent! Thus, there is room in the human brain for acquiring new kinds of information for many years after birth.

The baby chimp is quite strong and quick only a few days after it is born, and within a few weeks it begins to look for its own food. But the human baby is helpless for months, and it will be years before it can even begin to take care of itself. Yet this helplessness and the long period of child care that human offspring require are really an advantage, because they enable human beings to absorb far more information than any other animal. By the time the average human has reached adulthood, he or she is far more clever and knows much more than the wisest and most brilliant gorilla or chimpanzee.

Humans were not always as different from other animals as they are today. The first humans, for example, had brains that were only slightly larger than the brains of our smartest ape relatives, the chimps. In the beginning, humans used simple tools and stood erect, but in most other respects they lived very much like other animals. In the next three chapters, we will trace the history of our species as it evolved into the unusual and distinctive animal we are now. As you will see, the story of our evolution seems to have occurred in three stages. In the first stage, the first humans—walking upright and using stone tools—appeared. In the second stage, humans learned to use fire and to hunt large game. In the third stage, they became people like us.

IV THE FIRST HUMANS

Ramapithecus

The first animal that might possibly have been human lived as much as 20 or 25 million years ago. This creature is called "Ramapithecus." Almost everything we say about Ramapithecus is pure guesswork at this point, because the only remains that have ever been found of this mysterious animal are some teeth and some jaw fragments. Although this is not much evidence, there are good reasons for supposing that Ramapithecus was very close to being human.

The remains of Ramapithecus's canine teeth are particularly interesting to scientists. Like cats and dogs, apes and monkeys all have fairly large canine teeth. These teeth are their most important weapons. Among some species, such as baboons, the canine teeth are so long and sharp that an adult male baboon can fatally wound a full-grown leopard. We humans have short and blunt canine teeth, so we must *make* weapons for protecting ourselves and our offspring.

Like us, Ramapithecus had small, rounded canine teeth, clearly useless for fighting. In fact, the shape of Ramapithecus's jaw and entire set of teeth is amazingly similar to our own. This may mean that Ramapithecus ate the same kinds of foods we do. It may also mean that Ramapithecus used weapons to defend itself. Wild chimpanzees have been seen throwing rocks and waving sticks at their enemies. Why not Ramapithecus? And if Ramapithecus did use tools, perhaps he also walked upright in order to carry them about. If so, Ramapithecus would qualify as the oldest of all prehistoric humans.

At the present time, Ramapithecus is a scientific mystery. No one knows if this creature was really just an ape with teeth similar to ours, whether it was a true human who walked upright and used tools, or whether it was something in between. At one

THE FIRST HUMANS

A baboon bares its long and dangerous canine teeth.

site, scientists found some Ramapithecus remains along with the cracked-open bones and skulls of other animals. Did Ramapithecus crack these open to get at the marrow or the soft brains? Also found at this site was a lump of volcanic rock that looked as if it had been used for pounding or hammering. Was this one of Ramapithecus's stone tools? No one yet knows the answers to these puzzling questions.

Small-Brained Australopithecus and a Large-Brained Mystery

The earliest stone tools have been dated to about 3 million years ago; they were made by the first animal that we definitely know was human —an animal called "Australopithecus." Australopithecus stood and walked upright, and had a body almost exactly like ours, only smaller. Its brain, however, was not very much larger than the brain of a chimpanzee.

The first Australopithecus remains were found in a gorge in East Africa called "Olduvai." Thus, the distinctive kind of stone tools found with these remains are referred to as "Oldowan tools." Oldowan tools are usually made of large, rounded pebbles that have been pounded or struck with other stones so that several large chips are knocked off on both sides, forming a sharp, jagged edge. While these tools are crude compared to the stone tools that more advanced humans made later on, they would have been quite capable of chopping open the body of an animal killed in the hunt or cutting open the tough roots of edible wild plants.

In addition to the Oldowan remains, another discovery was made in East Africa that turned out to be one of the unsolved mysteries of prehistory. This was a skull and some leg bones that seem to have belonged to a prehistoric human who walked erect like Australopithecus but whose brain was much larger in size. Some scientists believe that these remains —which are from the same time period as Australopithecus — are evidence that "true" humans existed almost 3 million years ago and that it was they—not Australopithecus— who evolved into modern human beings.

So far, scientists have mostly reserved judgement about whether the small-brained Australopithecus or this mysterious large-brained human—whom we still know very little about—was the ancestor of our own species. And scientists are still not sure which of these two creatures made the pebble tools of that period. Actually, the Oldowan pebble tools are so crude that some of them look like stones that simply became broken from natural causes. This crudeness has always been explained as due to the fact that the small-brained Australopithecus simply was not smart enough to make good tools. If the tools turn out to be made by a large-brained human, prehistorians will have to come up with a different explanation.

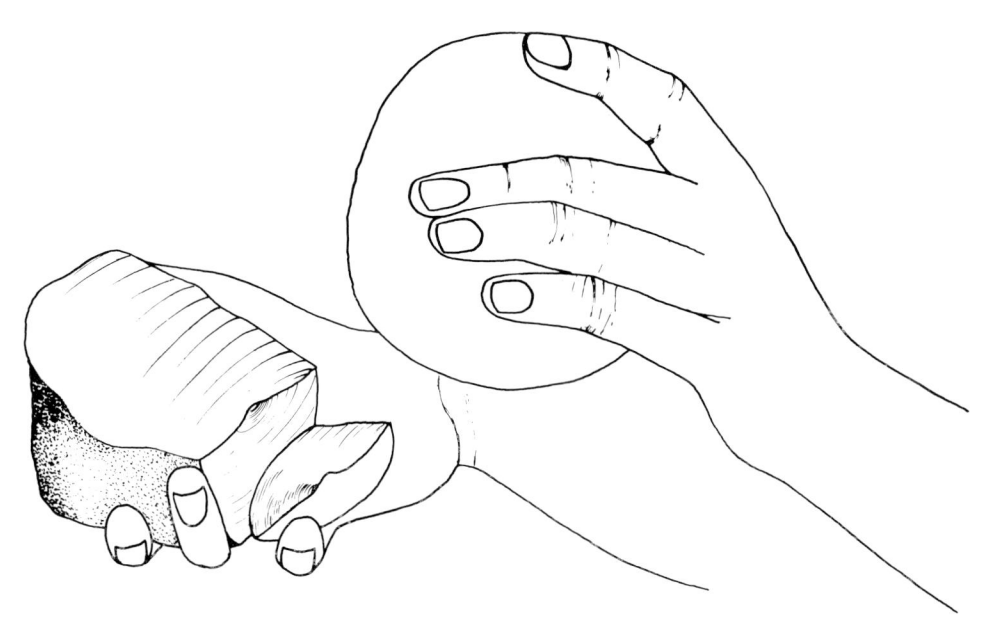

Striking a pebble with a hammerstone produces a flake.

Oldowan Tools

Regardless of their origin, the Oldowan pebble tools represent the first stone tools we know of that were deliberately made and used by any species of animal. These early tools show most of the basic characteristics of all stone tools. They were made by holding a stone in one hand and striking it with another stone in order to knock flakes off. If the flakes were knocked off at the correct angle on both sides of the pebble, a large, heavy chopping tool with a simple cutting edge could be produced. The flakes themselves were useful as fine cutting-tools, because their edges were sharper than those of the chopping tool.

But how do we know that these rough, jagged pieces of broken rock were really stone tools? Could it not be possible that, out of the hundreds and hundreds of stones found in a site, the archaeologists simply *chose* the ones that looked most like tools?

As the archaeologists themselves are the first to admit, it is possible to be mistaken about such things. Some of the objects that have been

THE FIRST HUMANS

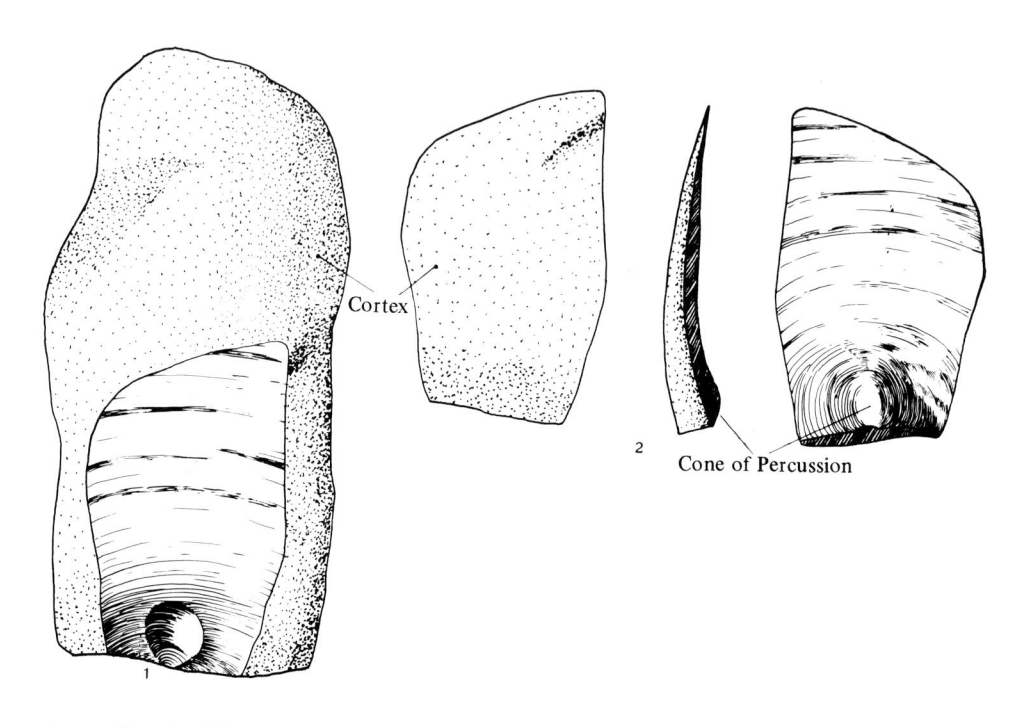

A core (1) and a flake struck from it (2). One side of the flake shows the cortex — the natural surface — of the core. The other side is marked with the cone-shaped bump and the ripples caused by a shock wave.

called "stone tools" may be, in fact, rocks that were naturally broken into a stone tool shape. But there are signs that help to distinguish real stone tools from pieces of broken rock. When a stone is taken and deliberately hit with another stone, the kind of break that results is different from the break that occurs naturally.

Have you ever seen a hole made in a window by a bullet or a BB pellet? If you have, you know that the hole is shaped like a cone. This is because when the fast-moving object strikes something hard, it produces a cone-shaped shock wave in the hard material. The break then occurs along the lines of the shock wave. Sometimes this shock wave also has small ripples in it, like the ripples formed on the surface of a quiet puddle or pond when you throw a stone into it.

When scientists examine the stones they dig out of an archaeological site, they look for the small cone-like bumps and ring-shaped ripples caused by the shock wave that results when a stone is deliberately struck with another stone. Such shock waves are almost never produced naturally, because the natural processes that cause stones to split apart occur too slowly for shock waves to form.

Another method that prehistorians use to determine whether an object is a stone tool is to examine its edges. They look for the characteristic marks indicating that the tool has been trimmed or retouched by having small pieces of stone knocked off its edges. If you pick up a stone (however rough in shape) that has a row of flakes knocked off it, and you see the signs of shock waves on the broken surfaces, then you can be sure it is a genuine stone tool.

The first humans used their crude Oldowan tools to do things that they could not do with their soft nails and small, rounded teeth. Although no objects of wood have survived from this time period, the first humans probably used pointed sticks for digging, hunting, and fighting. Chopping tools would have been useful for cutting branches, smashing the

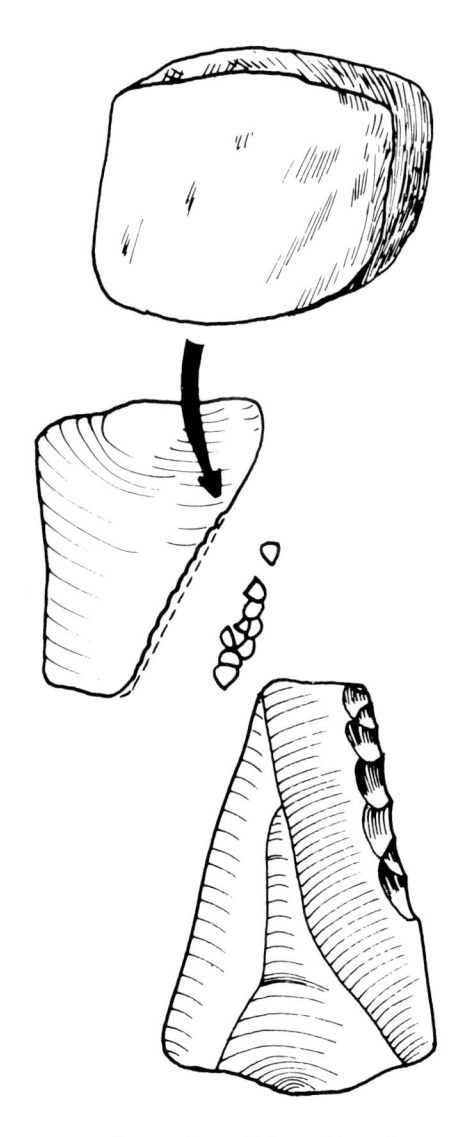

The process of retouching a flake tool by using a hammerstone to chip small fragments of stone off the edges

THE FIRST HUMANS

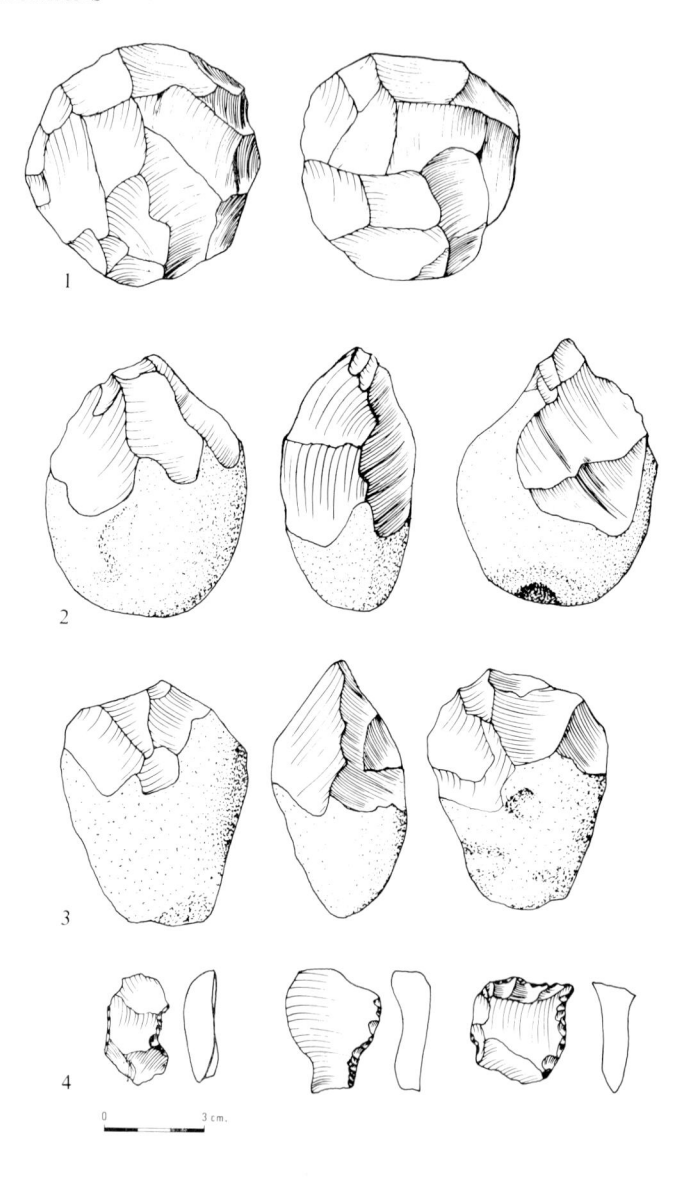

Major kinds of stone tools from the Oldowan period: 1) spheroids; 2–3) chopping tools; 4) primitive flake tools.

skulls and bones of game animals to get at the soft brains and marrow, and cutting away the strong tendons and ligaments, which could be used for tying or binding things together. Flake tools were probably used for cutting and scraping materials such as wood, bone, and animal skins.

In the last part of the Oldowan period, when the first humans had begun to improve the tools they made, round stones called "spheroids" began to appear. These stones were flaked all around into a spherical shape, and they were probably used as missiles. Thus the basic collection of tools from this earliest period of human life consisted mainly of two stone tools—the chopper and the flake—with a rather specialized stone weapon added at the very end. In time, this simple tool kit would be vastly improved and expanded by the generations of prehistoric humans who came after.

What Were the First Humans Like?

The first humans walked fully upright, as we do, but their bodies and brains were much smaller than ours. Australopithecus had a brain only about one-half the size of ours, while the large-brained human of the same period had a brain nearly two-thirds the size of our own. Both types of humans had small canine teeth, and both probably ate a diet of fruits, nuts, roots, berries, and meat, similar to the diet we eat today. (Some scientists have suggested that the larger-brained humans actually killed and ate their smaller-brained Australopithecus cousins!)

Although the first humans were hunters, most of the game they killed seems to have consisted of small animals, such as young antelopes and pigs. There are fewer remains of large animals like elephants, hippopotamuses, and giraffes found at these sites. (In fact, the first humans may not actually have hunted these large animals at all. They may simply have found them dead—perhaps killed by large predators, such as lions—and have dragged parts of them back to camp to eat in safety.) The remains of frogs, reptiles, and small rodents have also been found at prehistoric sites. From this evidence it is clear that the first humans hunted and killed a much greater variety of animals than any of our ape or monkey relatives.

One of the most important differences between these first humans and their ape-like ancestors is that the humans occupied a home base for days or weeks at a time, leaving during the day to hunt and gather

THE FIRST HUMANS

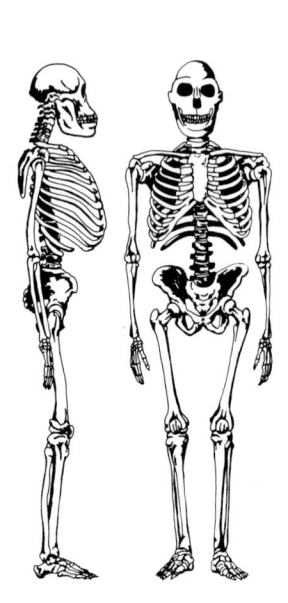

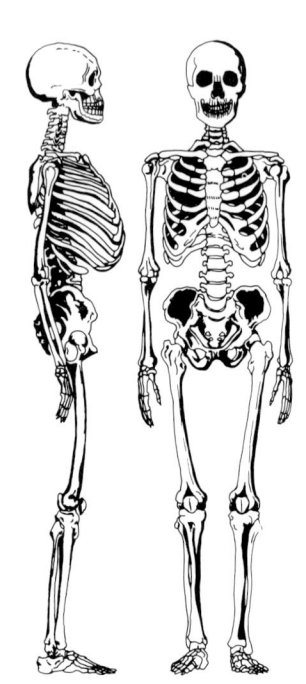

A reconstruction of the skeleton of Australopithecus (left) compared to the skeleton of a modern human being (right)

wild foods and returning at night to sleep in the safety of the group. Even more important, the humans brought much of their food back home with them to eat. On the other hand, apes usually wander about constantly, sleeping wherever they happen to be when night falls. When they find food, they sit down and eat it on the spot. Thus, while they usually gather together at night to sleep near each other, they do not have a home base in the sense that humans do.

Among chimps, it is the adult males who do almost all of the hunting, and the same was probably true of the first humans too. While the males hunted, the females probably gathered vegetable foods. Then, at the end of the day, all returned to the home base with the food they collected, and the members of the group probably shared their food with each other.

It is also possible that even at this early stage humans had begun to mature much more slowly, to require more care in childhood, and to *learn*

—through some kind of primitive language—how to live in the world. Other differences may have begun to develop as well. Among apes and monkeys, the sick and the aged are given no special care, but humans often give special care to the members of their group who are sick or old.

In the early stage of human development, the existence of a home base would have allowed weaker individuals to rest while the others hunted and gathered for the group. The ape or monkey group, constantly on the move, cannot do this. Thus, even in those early days, the bonds of love, tenderness, and sympathy that we think of as distinctively human may already have been forming among our first human ancestors.

The shaded section on the map shows the area in which remains from the Oldowan period have been found.

V   THE REVOLUTIONARY HUNTERS AND FIRE BUILDERS

About 1 million years ago, a new tool began to appear among the flakes and the chopping tools of the Oldowan culture. This tool was shaped like a pear, with two sharp edges that came together to form a point at the narrow end. The rounded end was meant to be held in the hand, and thus the new tool was called a "handaxe." At first, handaxes were small and somewhat crude, but as time passed, they became more finely made and also more common. Eventually, they replaced the chopper as the most important stone tool of prehistoric times.

*Homo Erectus and the
New Stone Tools*

The change from chopping tool to handaxes was a major advance in human culture. While it took some intelligence and manual skill to knock a few large flakes off a pebble and make a chopping tool, it took craftsmanship, patience, and probably a great deal of practice to make a fine handaxe. Clearly, this was not the work of a creature with a brain slightly larger than that of a chimpanzee.

The new handaxe culture is called "Acheulian," and the fossil remains that are found with it are those of a new and different type of human, with a brain that ranged up to twice the size of the Australopithecus brain. This new human is called *Homo erectus.*

Homo erectus spread throughout the Old World, traveling far from the old Australopithecus homeland and the plains of Africa. The remains of *Homo erectus,* and of the Acheulian handaxe culture that this creature used, have been found not only in Africa but all across Europe and Asia as well, from France to China and even to Southeast Asia.

For reasons that no one understands, *Homo erectus* did not seem to make any handaxes in lands east of India. In China and other parts of the Orient, the remains of *Homo erectus* are found with the tools of the ancient Oldowan tradition.

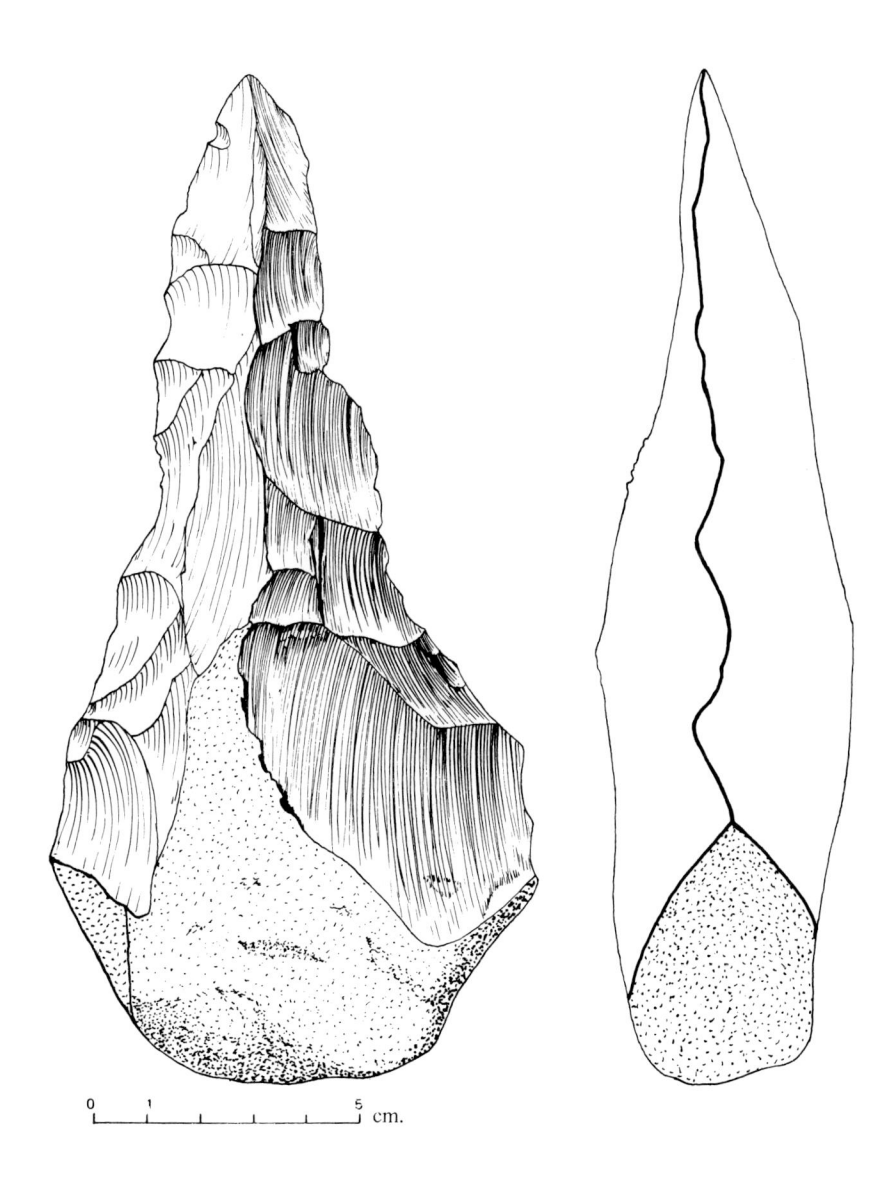

A handaxe seen from the front and the side.

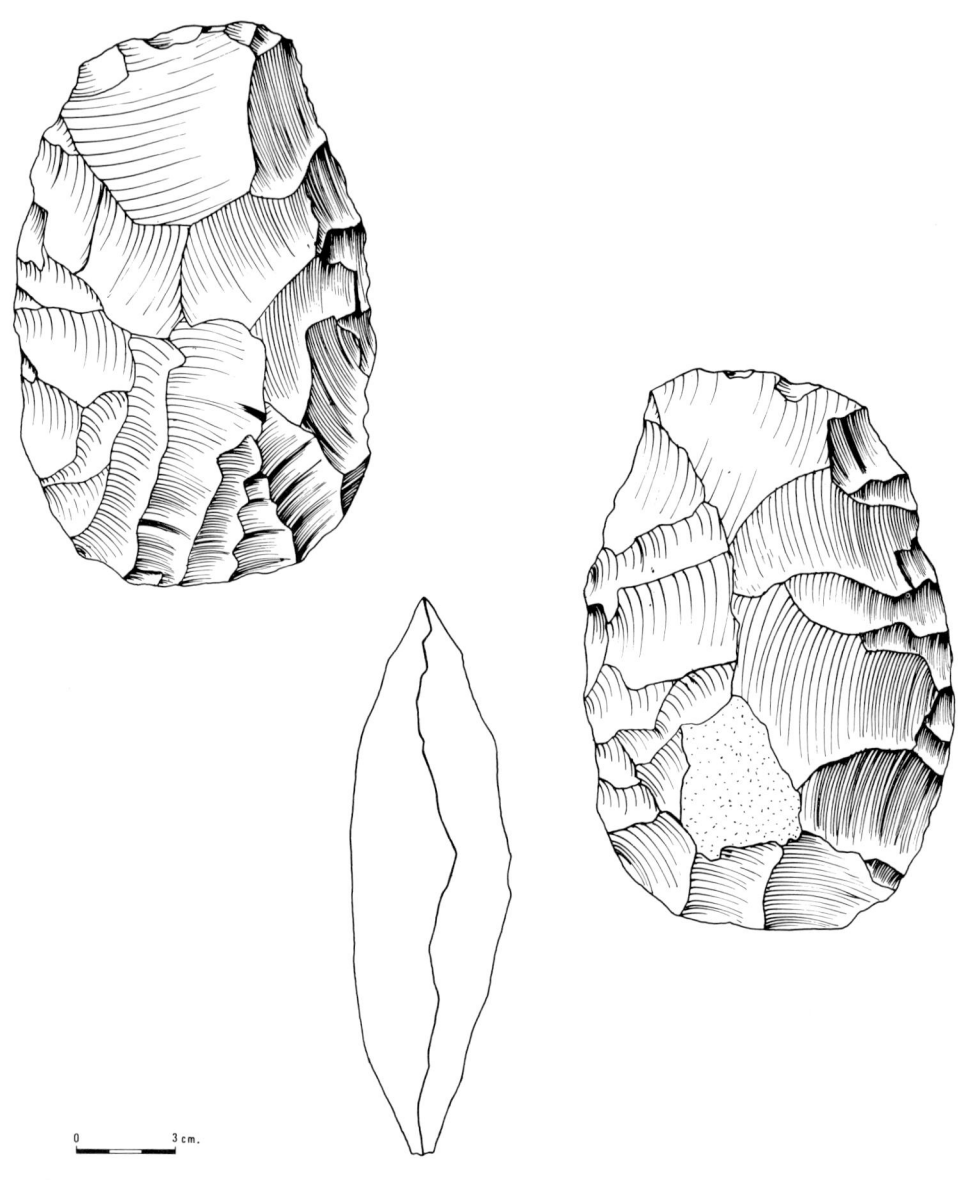

A cleaver shown from the front, the side, and the back.

While all other populations of *Homo erectus* did make and use handaxes, there was still much variation in the tool kit from one region to another. The clearest example of this variation occurs in Africa, where *Homo erectus* was especially fond of a tool known as a "cleaver," which is a handaxe with a straight cutting edge rather than a pointed one. In some of these African sites, more than half of the handaxes are of the cleaver type, while elsewhere cleavers are rare.

At the beginning of the Acheulian tool tradition, handaxes were made in a variety of shapes and sizes, but as time went on, *Homo erectus* began making handaxes with increasingly similar forms. At the same time, the amount of work needed to make each handaxe increased greatly. While only 10 flakes needed to be removed to make a chopping tool, between 100 and 200 flakes had to be removed to make one of the beautiful pear-shaped handaxes that *Homo erectus* eventually learned how to make.

In addition to handaxes, *Homo erectus* invented a whole group of tools that the Australopithecines had never even attempted to make. While the Oldowan tool kit was mainly limited to either chopping tools or crude flakes, the Acheulian tool kit contained not only handaxes and cleavers but also scrapers, notchers, knives, awls for boring holes, and other specialized flake tools designed for working in wood, bone, and leather. Many of these tools were produced by striking the stone not with another stone but with a hammer made of wood or bone. This produced a softer impact, and the resulting flakes could be removed more precisely.

Although only their stone tools have survived to the present day, the humans of Acheulian times must have made many other things requiring skill, patience, and coordination. Most important of all, they made things that required the ability to communicate complex information and to pass on traditions from one generation to the next. It is in this stage of human history— between roughly 1 million and 200,000 years ago — that the clear evidence of culture and tradition first appears. *Homo erectus* was probably the first human to use a system of communication that we would call "language."

There are many differences between the first humans of the Oldowan tradition and these new humans of the Acheulian handaxe tradition, but probably the most important difference of all is that the Acheulian people were strong, efficient, and daring hunters. While the first humans were content to live mainly off of young and helpless pigs and antelopes, *Homo erectus* hunted giraffes, elephants, wild cattle, giant baboons, and giant antelopes. They even pursued the fearsome sabertoothed tiger, a lion-sized animal with canine teeth so long they projected down below its jaws like walrus's tusks. In fact, scientists who study the remains of prehistoric wildlife have recently suggested that such creatures disappeared because *Homo erectus* and his descendants actually hunted them to extinction!

The Mastery of Fire

The oldest evidence of fire that has ever been found comes from a cave in southern France. This evidence is about 750,000 years old and dates from a period well after the time at which Australopithecus disappeared. Unless some new and much older proof of the deliberate use of fire by humans is discovered, it seems clear that it was *Homo erectus* who first learned to use and control fire. This is something that no other animal ever did before, and it marks one of the most important milestones in the evolution of our species.

Up to that time, the achievements of early humans had been mainly a continuation and improvement of the achievements of other animals. Chimpanzees use simple tools, wolves cooperate in hunting, and many animals—from mice to porpoises—have systems of communication involving the use of sounds. But the control of fire was not simply an improvement of an ability already possessed by other animals. It was a revolutionary achievement on a totally different level, and it established a separation between humans and other animals that has only widened and deepened with the passage of time.

Since all animals besides humans are frightened of fire, the early humans could use fire to protect themselves. By building a fire and staying near it, they could create a place of safety that no other animal would dare to violate. *Homo erectus* also discovered that by setting fire to dry grasslands or dry bush country, wild game could be stampeded in the direction of a cliff, a sticky swamp, or a group of hunters. Thus the animals could be killed easily in larger number than ever before. Finally, some prehistorians believe that humans were able to migrate out of their African homeland and settle the cooler lands of Europe and Asia to the north because they had learned to make fire and carry it with them as they moved about.

Besides providing protection from wild animals, assistance in the hunt, and warmth in cold climates, fire enabled humans to do something else never attempted by any other animal, namely, to cook food. We take cooking for granted, and in fact almost every known human society uses fire to cook at least some of its food. But in this activity too, we stand alone in the animal kingdom. The discovery of cooking brought about a significant change in the human diet by enlarging and expanding the range of foods humans could eat. Because of this development, many foods that could not be digested when raw became staples in the human diet.

Perhaps one of the most interesting side-effects of the use of fire was the change that it brought about in the shape of the human face. This change took place because the food that humans learned to cook over their fires required much less chewing than raw food. With less need for chewing, the size of human teeth decreased greatly over a period of time. Thus, while the brain was expanding, causing the forehead to bulge outward, the teeth were shrinking, causing the mouth to collapse inward. (Smaller teeth take up less room in the mouth, and they require smaller lips to keep them covered.) This shrinking in of the mouth region is responsible for our small, short lips, our pointed noses, and our sharp chins, all of which are opposites of the flat noses, the long, large lips, and the nonexistent chins of the typical ape or monkey face. The use of fire changed us in many ways, but this must surely be the strangest!

It must have been during this period of human history that our ancestors developed the special affection for fires and fireplaces that we have retained to this day. When the fireplace became the center of warmth, of safety, and of food, it must have also become the focus of group activity. All the members of the group probably gathered around the fire in the evening to discuss the activities and discoveries of the day, to recall the adventures and experiences of the past, and to make plans for the day to come. Thus, the fire would have served not only as a place where adults would exchange information, but also as a place

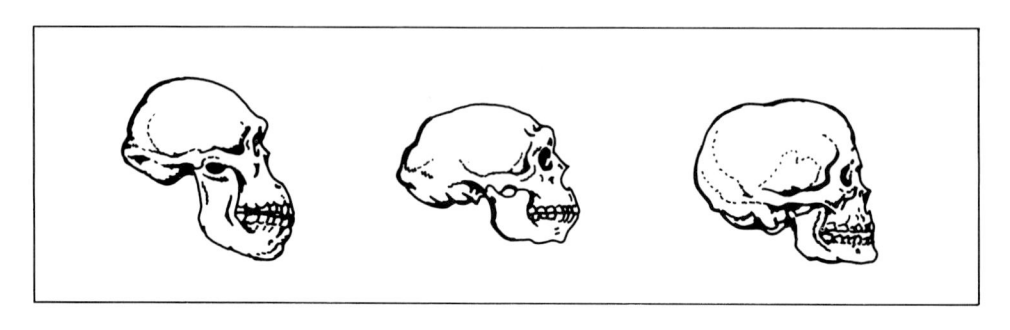

Left to right: Drawings of the skulls of Australopithecus, *Homo erectus,* and *Homo sapiens* showing the gradual changes in the shape of the human face

where the young could absorb this information.

Finally, the control of fire changed the position of humans in the natural world from equal participants—who hunted other animals and were hunted by them in return—to an all-but-unconquerable species that was feared by all animals and hunted by none (except by other humans). All this must have given *Homo erectus* quite a lot to think about.

Homo erectus, who probably gave us prowess in the hunt, skill in workmanship, the use of fire, the beginning of human language, and our distinctively human faces, disappeared about 200,000 years ago. The next human to appear was our own species, *Homo sapiens.*

VI PEOPLE LIKE US

About 250,000 years ago, people with brains as large as our own appeared. Gradually, these new humans increased in number, and *Homo erectus* began to disappear. Since very few remains from this time period have been found, we know little about the people who lived in those years of transition. By 150,000 years ago, the transition was complete. From this time on, the earth has been inhabited entirely by humans of our own species, *Homo sapiens*.

Life After Death

At first, our *Homo sapiens* ancestors carried on the Acheulian tool tradition of the *Homo erectus* people from whom they descended. But the handaxes and other tools that they made were more perfect and more beautiful than any stone tools made before that time. In fact, some of these handaxes are made so perfectly that we cannot help but think that prehistoric people of that time must have appreciated fine workmanship not just because it produced a better tool but also because it made an object more pleasing to see and touch. Perhaps this represents the first evidence of the human appreciation of beauty for its own sake.

Additional evidence can be seen in a find recently made in France—a bone decorated with a pattern of fine lines that had been inscribed on the surface with a stone tool. This bone, which dates from about 130,000 years ago, is probably the oldest object of art in existence. Some prehistorians believe that the new human appreciation of beauty and striving for perfection shows that, from the beginning, *Homo sapiens* people were able to think about—and fear—their own deaths. According to this theory, an awareness and fear of death led *Homo sapiens* to want to create objects of lasting beauty that would survive after their makers had ceased to exist. This theory fits well with one of the most interesting facts

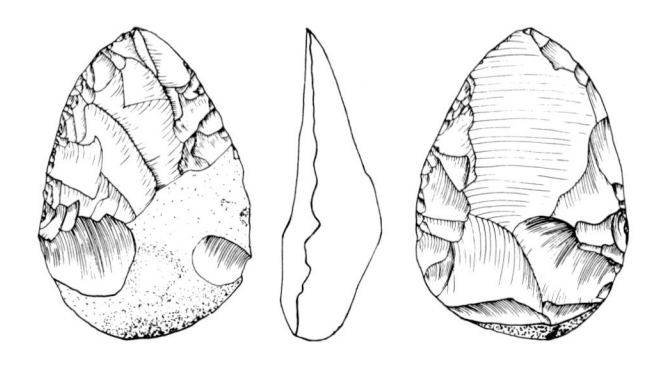

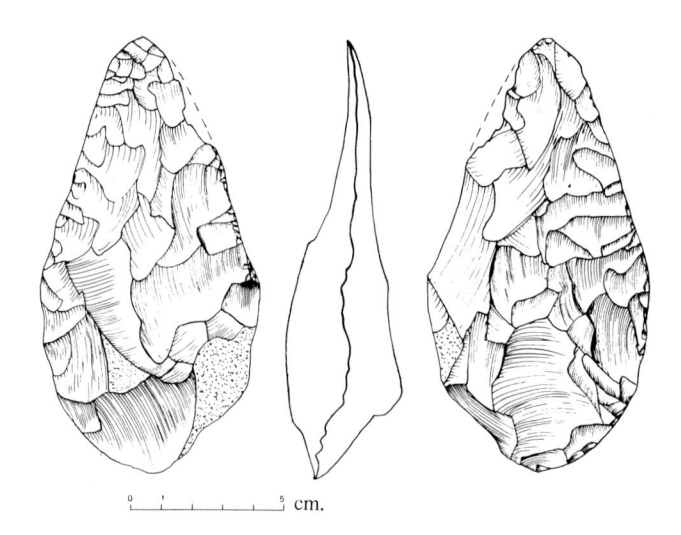

Above: Beautifully shaped handaxes from the late Acheulian period.

Right: This bone fragment inscribed with a pattern of fine lines is the oldest object of art known. It was found by archaeologists at Pech de L'Azé in France.

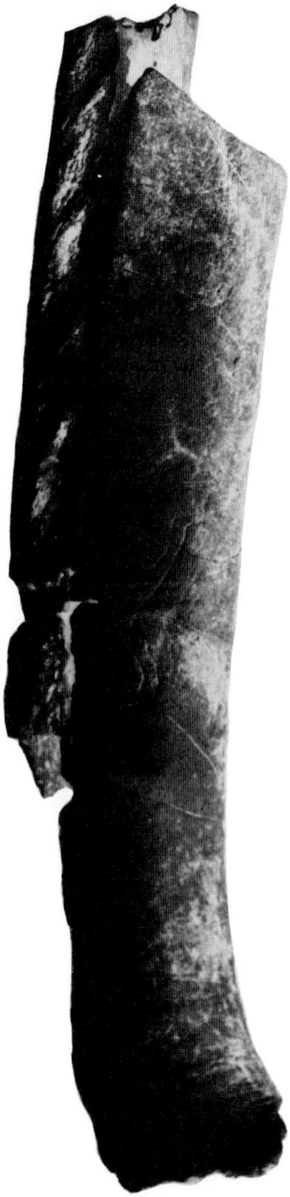

about these people: unlike any other humans before them, they buried their dead.

Beginning about 75,000 years ago, people all over the world began to dig graves and bury the members of their societies who had died. Their reason for burying the dead was not to protect the living members of the group from disease but rather to keep the deceased at home even after death. These graves were not dug in some distant cemetery or even in a nearby field or forest. They were dug in the floors of the huts and caves that the people were living in. Burying your dead relatives in the floor of your kitchen or living room might seem a bit strange to us, but if you believe that a person's spirit continues to live after death, it would be a normal and natural thing to do.

These prehistoric graves were small by our standards, consisting only of a round hole cut into the earth. The corpse was placed into this hole in a curled-up position, with the arms and legs bent. One of the clearest indications that *Homo sapiens* believed in life after death was that various kinds of material goods were put into the grave along with the corpse, probably to help the deceased survive in the afterlife. Graves from this period contain food, tools, and animal horns; in one grave the dead person had even been given a bouquet of flowers.

Sometimes a slab of stone was placed on top of the corpse before the grave was covered with earth, and in many cases the entire grave site was smeared with a red earth pigment called "ochre." Thus, from the beginning, burying the dead seems to have involved ceremony and ritual.

Cave Dwellers and Their Tools

Earlier in this book we mentioned that the Neanderthals were the first prehistoric humans to be discovered by modern science. Neanderthal skeletons look different from modern human skeletons, and for a long time we and the Neanderthals were believed to represent two different species of human being. But we now understand that — compared to the remains of Australopithecus and other early humans — the Neanderthals were really very much like ourselves. (For one thing, the Neanderthal brain was every bit as large as our own.) Scientists now agree that we and the Neanderthals are all members of the same species, *Homo sapiens*.

The people of 75,000 years ago who made those beautiful stone tools

This ancient burial found in Israel is about 50,000 years old. A pair of antlers was placed in the grave as an offering for the dead.

and who buried their dead were Neanderthals. More than most prehistoric people, the Neanderthals seemed to prefer living in caves and rock shelters whenever possible. These are the people we are referring to when we talk about "cave men." Although they are usually portrayed as sloppy and unwashed folks who carried huge wooden clubs and dragged their women around by the hair, they were really much more intelligent and refined than these popular ideas about them would indicate.

While living Neanderthals must have been somewhat different in appearance from the average person alive today, these differences were probably less obvious than you might think. If you could go back to prehistoric times and persuade a Neanderthal to return with you to the present, you could dress him up in modern clothes, put him in the middle of any town or city in the United States, and no one would know the difference. In fact, there is evidence that Neanderthals never really died out but simply interbred with the modern type of *Homo sapiens* that appeared later on. There are some people living today who are built just like Neanderthals, and even the experts would probably have trouble telling their skeletons apart from some Neanderthal remains, if it were not for the effects of time on the appearance of the bones themselves. Most of us probably have a little Neanderthal ancestry somewhere in our ancient family trees!

When the Neanderthals spread northward into the colder regions of Europe and Asia, they proved themselves better able to cope with cold weather than any humans before them. This may have been partly due to their choice of caves and rock shelters as dwelling-places (and it is certainly also due to their use of fire). But, even more important, Neanderthal people are known to have used animal skins for shelter, and they probably made clothing out of skins as well. This was yet another step that no animal had ever taken before. There is no other warm-blooded creature, bird or mammal, that kills other animals and wraps itself in their skins to keep warm.

The Neanderthals made some important improvements on the Acheulian tool kit, although they gradually stopped making handaxes and concentrated on making flake-tools and points for weapons. While they continued to use the hunting methods developed during the time of *Homo erectus,* they tended to choose one particular animal to hunt in preference to others. (Which animal this happened to be varied from one region to another.) Perhaps it was through learning to depend on one kind of animal for meat, hides, bone, and sinew that prehistoric people first had the idea of taming animals and purposely raising them to supply their needs.

Right: The image of a bison engraved on a bone, from La Madeleine in France. This work of art is about 15,000 years old.

Overleaf left: These sculpted and decorated pieces of amber were made 10,000 years ago.

Overleaf right: Stonehenge, a huge monument dating from the prehistoric period in England. Some archaeologists think that the structure may have been used as an astronomical observatory.

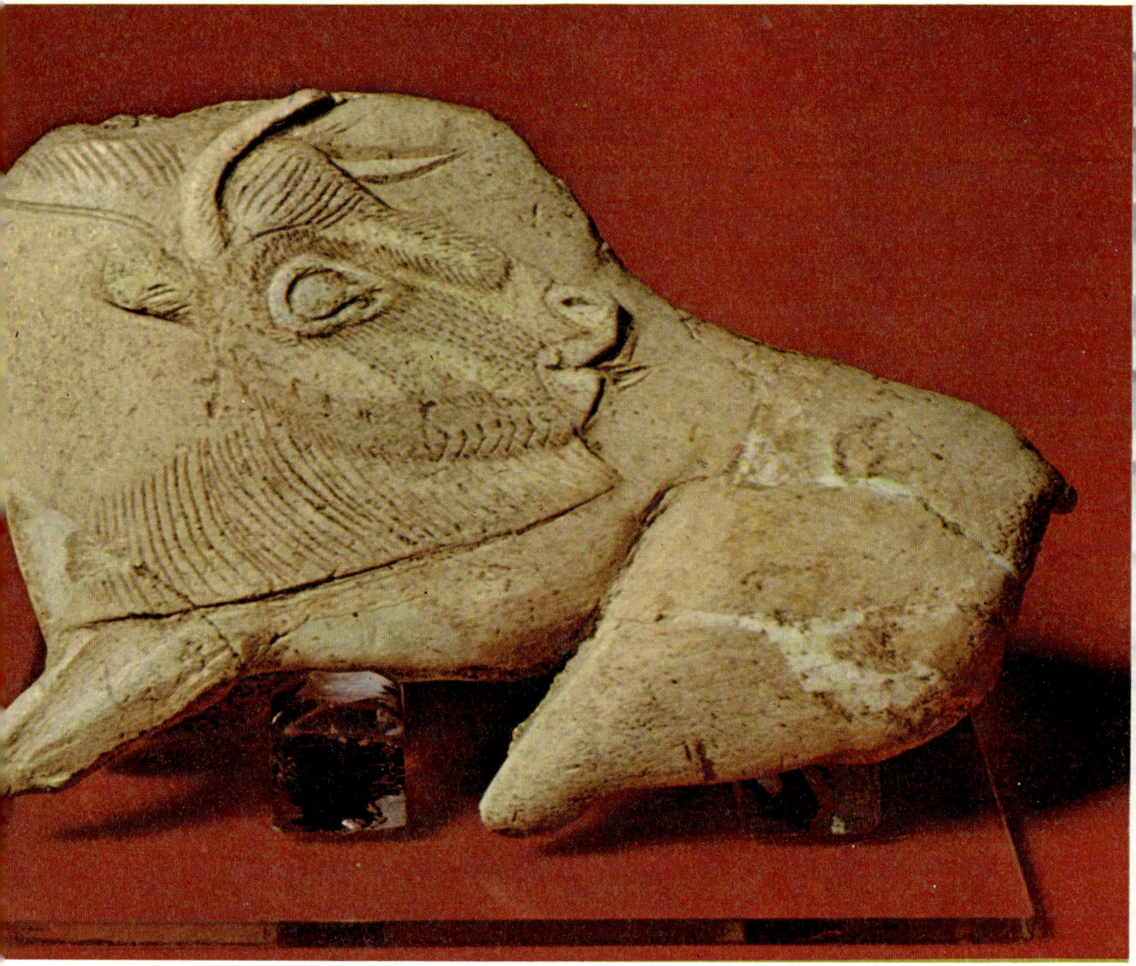

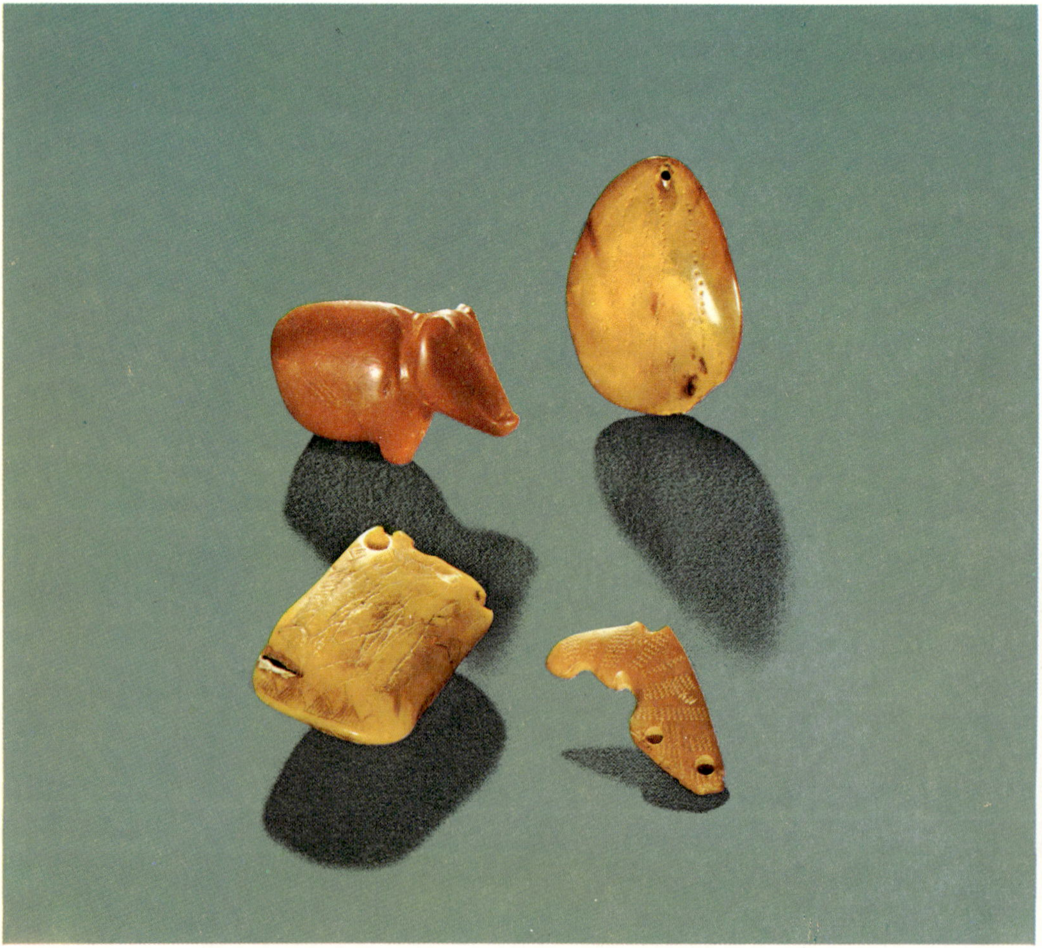

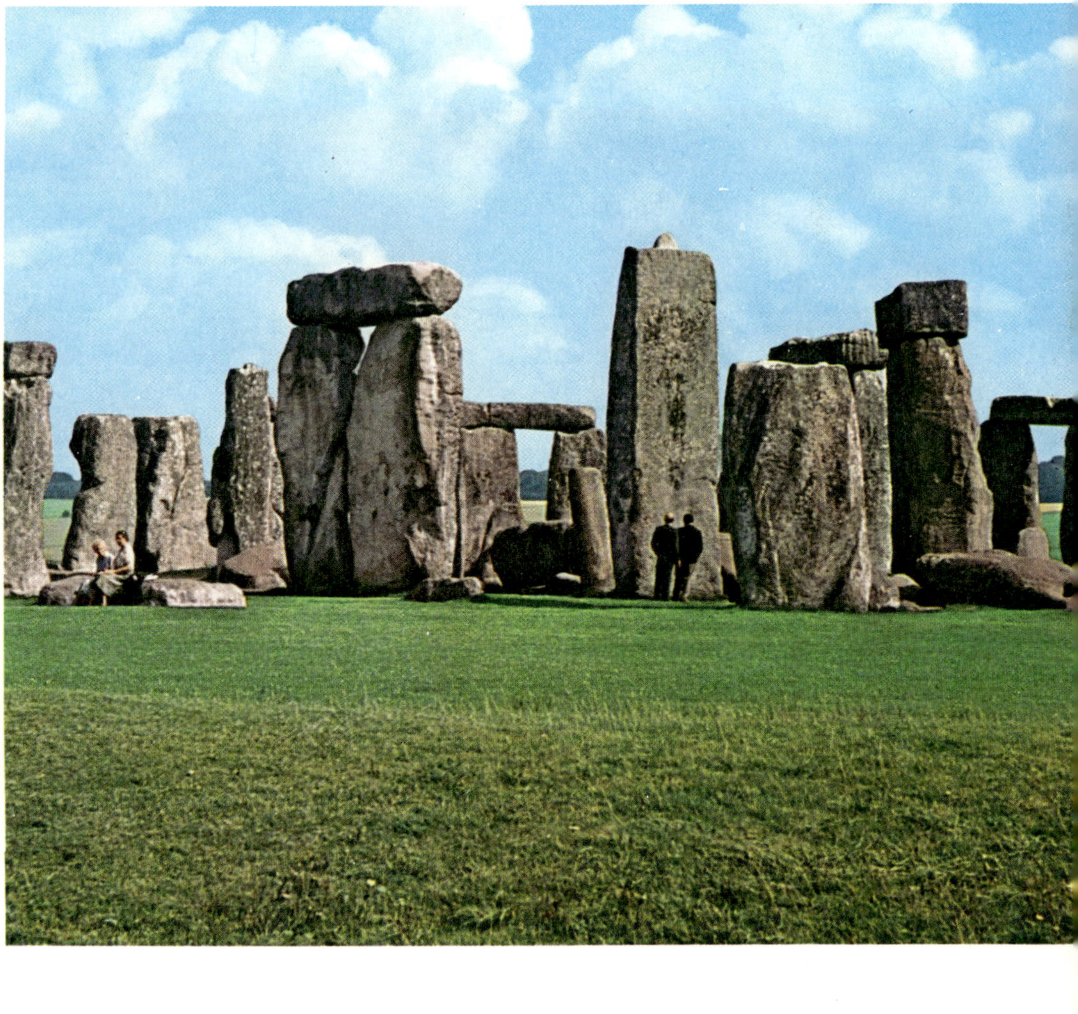

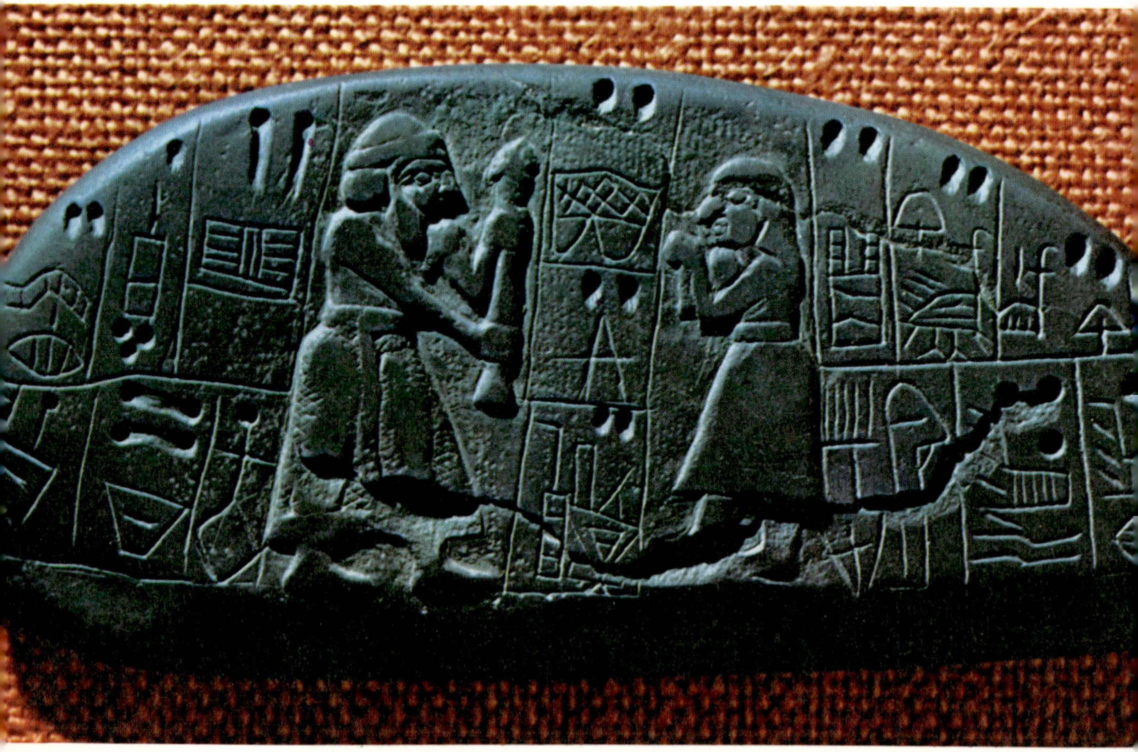

PEOPLE LIKE US

Above: The shaded section on the map indicates the area occupied by humans from about 1 million to 40,000 years ago.

Left: This pictographic inscription from Mesopotamia is an example of an early form of writing. When people learned to write and to keep written records, the prehistoric period came to an end.

Modern People and Their Arts

Sometime between 40,000 and 30,000 years ago, fully modern people began to appear in various parts of the Old World. There were still many Neanderthals, and modern people—who are sometimes called "Cro-Magnons" by prehistorians—mingled with them, perhaps even intermarrying with them to a great extent. Like the Neanderthals, Cro-Magnon people buried their dead, but they did something else as well, which no humans had ever really done before: they began to create works of art.

Suddenly, about 30,000 years ago, the world blossomed with the new artistic talents of prehistoric people.

74

Above: A piece of bone engraved with a pattern of lines and dots, found at Lartet, France. Archaeologists believe that the pattern represents the various phases of the moon.

Left: Front and side views of the figurine of a woman, carved in mammoth ivory. This figurine, which is about 34,000 years old, is the oldest known representation of the human form.

They made paintings on the sides of rocks and on the walls of caves, they made sculptures out of stone, ivory, bone, and clay, they engraved pictures and designs on the surfaces of rocks, bones, and antlers, and they made ornaments to decorate the human body. Most of this art consists of representations of plants, animals, and people, but archaeologists have also found curious symbolic notations as well. No one is certain what the purpose or meaning of these symbols really was, but certain ones may have served as calendars, others may have represented primitive methods of counting, and still others may even have represented a crude type of written language.

One of the most curious types of art from this period are the many statuettes of the female body called "Venus figurines." The heads, arms, and legs of these figurines are small and simplified, while the breasts, buttocks, and genitals are huge in proportion to the rest of the body. Thus they were probably meant to signify sex and fertility (see color plates).

Precision in Stone Tools

The modern people of prehistoric times developed two important new methods of making stone tools, and they produced the most perfectly fashioned tools ever made. The first of these methods involved the use of a tool called a "punch." Instead of striking the stone directly with a hammer, modern people discovered how to hold the point of a piece of bone or antler against the stone and then strike the other end of this punch with a stone hammer. This technique made it possible to strike the surface of the stone in *exactly* the place desired, instead of the old method of taking aim and hoping for the best.

The second improvement involved heating the stone in a fire, which made it possible to finish the tool by a method called "pressure flaking." Instead of striking the hot stone with a hammer, a hard, pointed object like a punch was simply pressed against the edge of the stone until a tiny flake popped off. In this way, the tool-makers could remove the small irregularities in a newly made tool, or they could shape extremely thin flakes into fine tools and weapons.

Using the punch, modern people learned how to make long, straight flakes with incredibly sharp edges. Archaeologists call these "blades." In fact, these long flakes are about the same size and shape as the blade of an old-fashioned straight razor. With the use of pressure flaking, the blades could be shaped into knives, spear points, arrowheads, and fine

A 25,000-year-old Venus figurine found in Czechoslovakia

tools for working in wood, bone, and ivory.

The modern people of prehistoric times brought their art, religion, symbolism, and highly advanced stone tool cultures to all regions of the earth. They migrated out of the Old World into Australia, the Pacific Islands, and the Americas, and they learned to survive in burning deserts, thick jungles, and the frozen Arctic. Each region of the earth was inhabited by different kinds of tribes, and each tribe developed its own artistic traditions, burial customs, and stone tool types. The stone tools of each regional group, in fact, are usually so distinctive that archaeologists can identify each prehistoric group by the distinctive shape of its own particular stone tool culture.

These hunting and gathering people, physically identical to ourselves, developed the hunting and gathering way of life — and the stone and bone tools and weapons on which it depended — to its most advanced state. In many ways, this was the climax of the stone age. Before long, people began to keep herds of animals and to grow crops. As they began to settle down, they had less use for fine hunting weapons and more need for the tools of farmers and herding people.

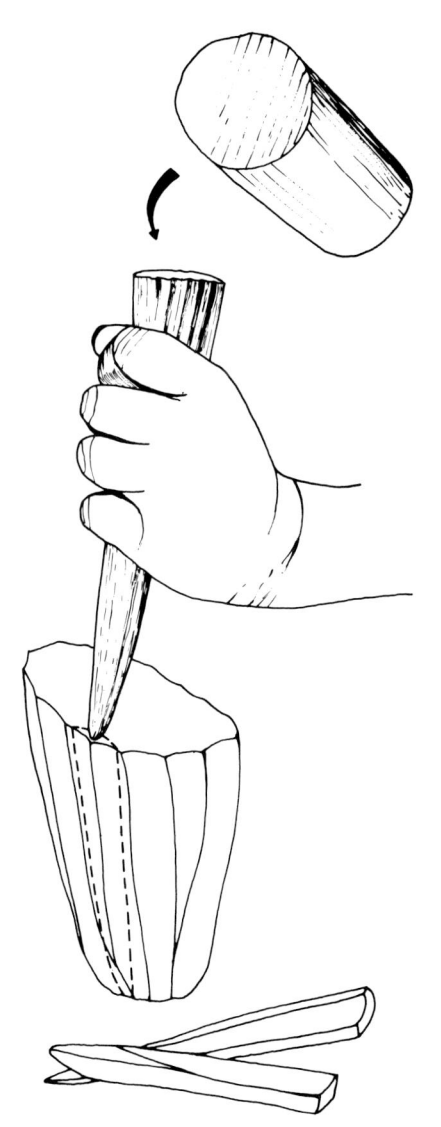

The process of making stone blades with the use of a punch.

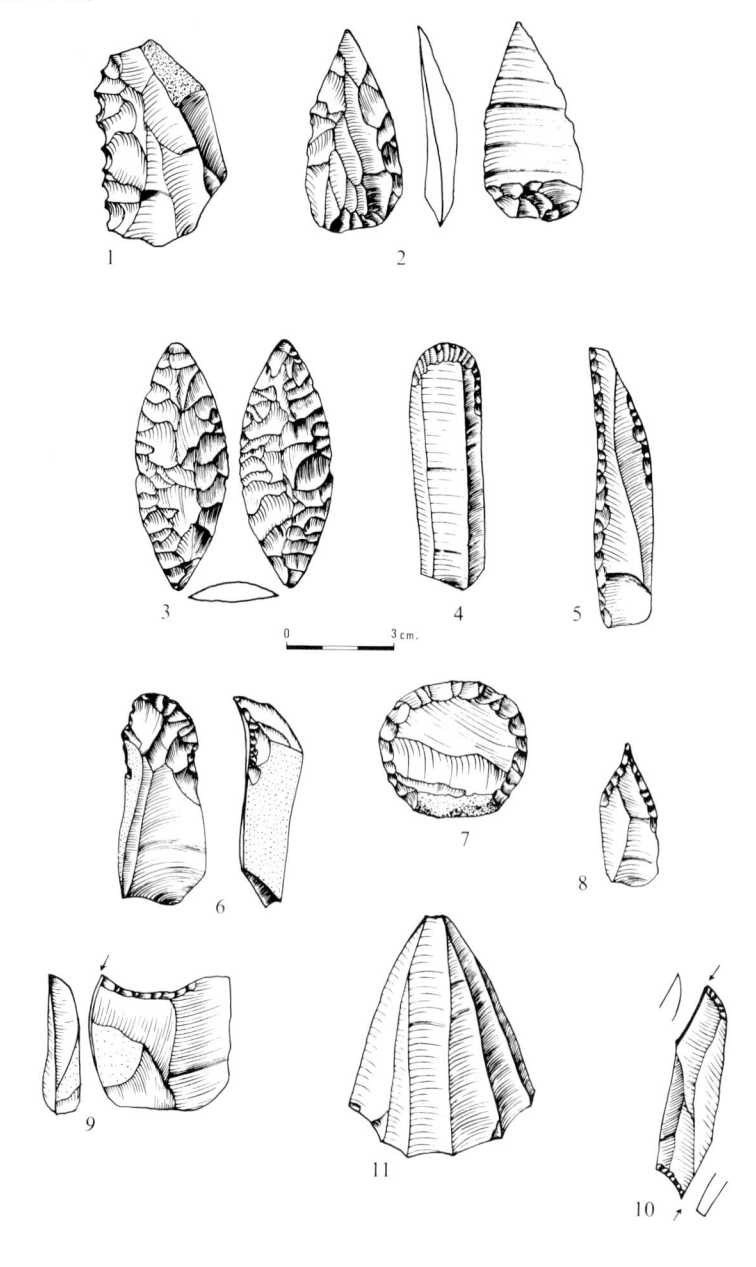

PEOPLE LIKE US

78

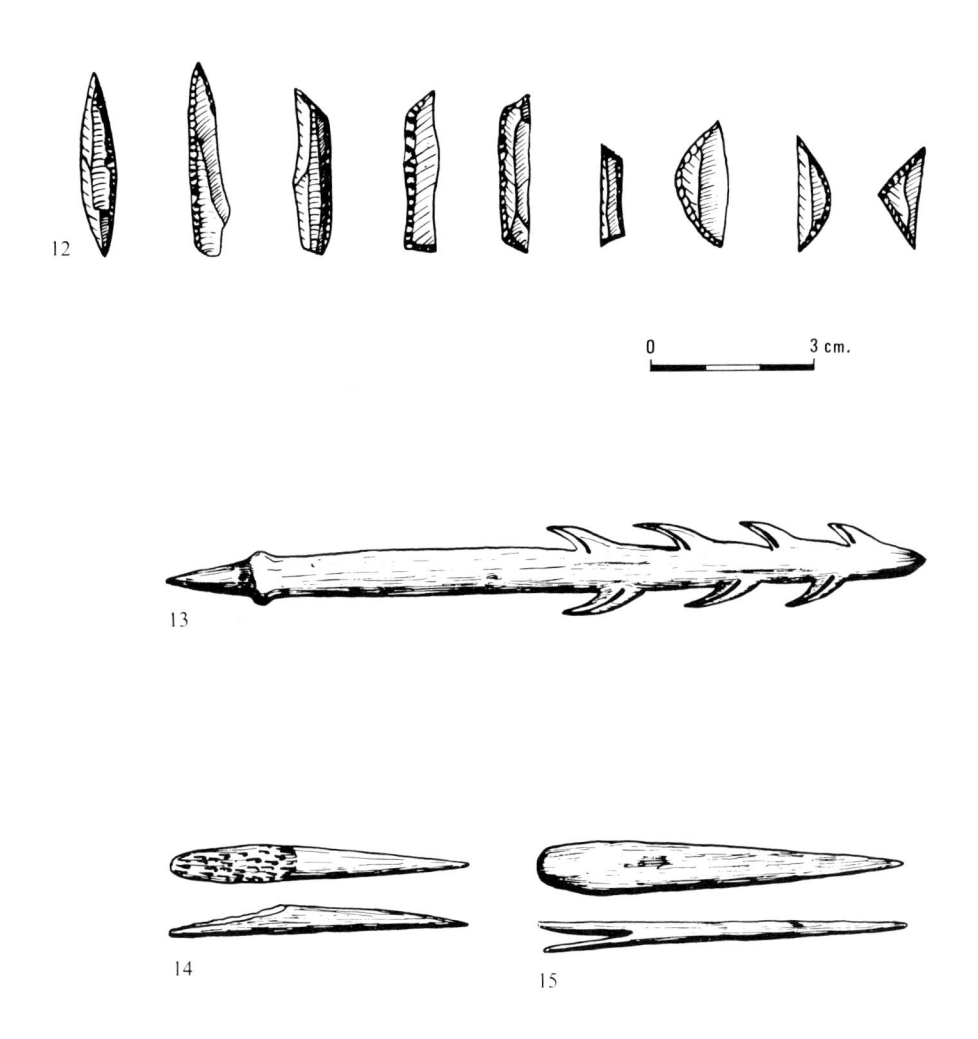

Left and above: Typical tools from the time period between 40,000 and 20,000 years ago: 1) a denticulated tool (a tool with teeth-like notches); 2-3) points; 4-7) scrapers; 8) an awl; 9-10) engravers; 11) a blade core; 12) microliths, or tiny stone tools; 13-15) bone points.

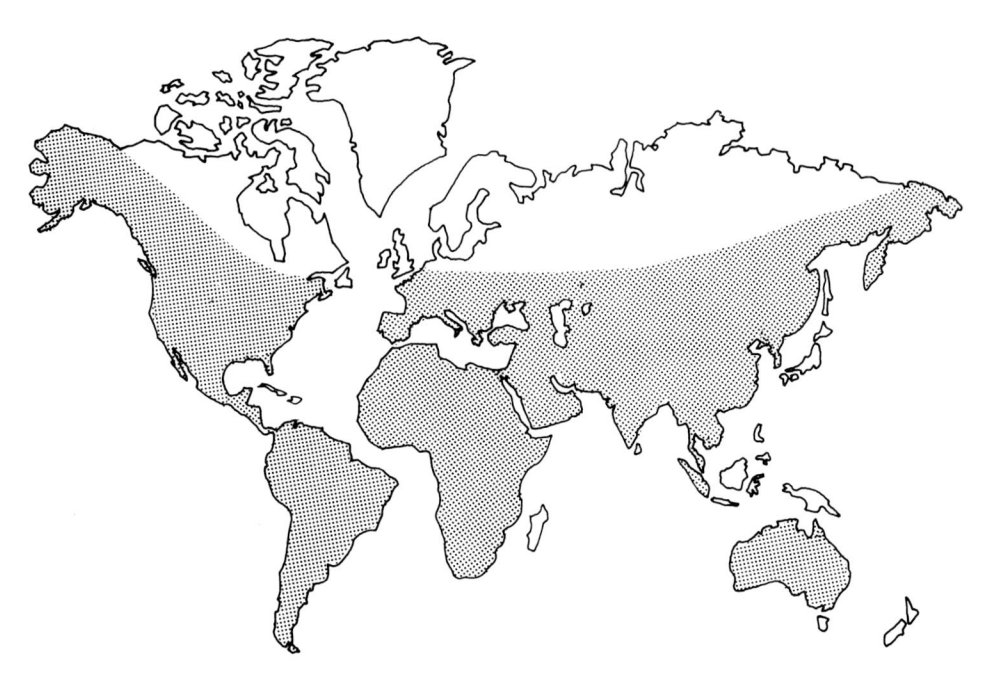

The shaded section on the map indicates the area inhabited by human beings 30,000 years ago.

VII THE DAWN OF HISTORY

As human beings became more skilled at hunting and more efficient at gathering vegetable foods, their numbers began to increase. And since humans had already learned to use fire and weapons to defend themselves against any natural predators, it is easy to see why the earth's human population continued to increase with the passage of time. *Homo sapiens* spread throughout the entire earth, moving into lands that no humans had ever inhabited before, such as North and South America. But even in prehistoric times, people faced the problem of overpopulation.

As time passed, wild foods of all kinds became more and more scarce. Many animal species probably became extinct as a result of being hunted too successfully by our prehistoric ancestors. As times grew hard, people learned to cooperate more, to make better tools, and to exploit the environment more fully.

But however efficient people became at getting wild food, there was simply not enough of it to go around. Any other animal species, faced with a dwindling food supply and an expanding population, eventually reaches the point where mass starvation and death occur. This drastically reduces the population and thus insures enough food for the few survivors to grow, prosper, and repeat the cycle again and again. Such mass deaths due to overpopulation are constantly occurring in nature among a wide variety of animal species.

By the time that overpopulation threatened prehistoric human beings, however, they were no longer just another species of animal. They had developed tools and weapons, language, group cooperation, and the ability to contemplate the future and to make plans for dealing with future problems. So our ancestors began to experiment, trying new ways of getting food from the land. Eventually, they learned how to produce their

PEOPLE LIKE US

Archaeologists found a skeleton wearing a headband made of sea shells in this 12,000-year-old grave in Israel.

own food by raising animals and growing crops.

This change from food-gathering to food-producing resulted in a total transformation of human life, often referred to as the "agricultural revolution." But this name is misleading, because it implies that the domestication of plants and animals took place quite suddenly. There was, in fact, no sudden change but rather a slow and laborious process by which people learned which plants and animals could be tamed and how to take care of them.

The Ancient Grain Belt

There is a stretch of land running eastward from the Mediterranean Sea that has an ideal climate and soil for wild grains. This natural grain belt of prehistoric times gave people the first important opportunity to learn how to grow their own food. About 15,000 years ago, the people who lived in this part of the world had begun to use a mortar and pestle for grinding grain. While these people may not yet have learned to grow the grain themselves, it is clear that they had found a way to use this abundant natural resource as food.

At about the same time, the population of the ancient grain belt seems to have been growing; archaeologists have also found evidence that the people of the area were settling down to live in villages. It was not long before these people began making sickles for harvesting the wild grain. By 12,000 years ago, they had developed a way of life based on gathering, storing, grinding, and cooking cereal grain.

Then, about 10,000 years ago, a very important event took place. The wild grain—and some wild species of goats and sheep—began to appear in regions far from their original habitat. Something—or someone—was transporting these plants and animals to new locations. It seems almost certain that prehistoric people were responsible for this activity. Such evidence indicates that by 10,000 years ago, our ancestors had finally learned how to plant and harvest crops and how to keep herds of animals for their own use.

By 8,000 years ago, these plants and animals had developed new strains that were different from the wild forms. The process of domestication was complete. Soon, people in other parts of the world learned to grow their own grain and raise their own animals. Agriculture was invented independently in at least two other parts of the world in addition to the ancient Middle East: in

THE DAWN OF HISTORY 84

This mortar and pestle, the oldest of its kind ever found, is about 15,000 years old.

the Far East, people learned how to grow rice, and in the Americas, people learned how to grow corn. Once humans had gotten the *idea* of raising their own food, they found many species of wild plants and animals that could be tamed and domesticated for human use.

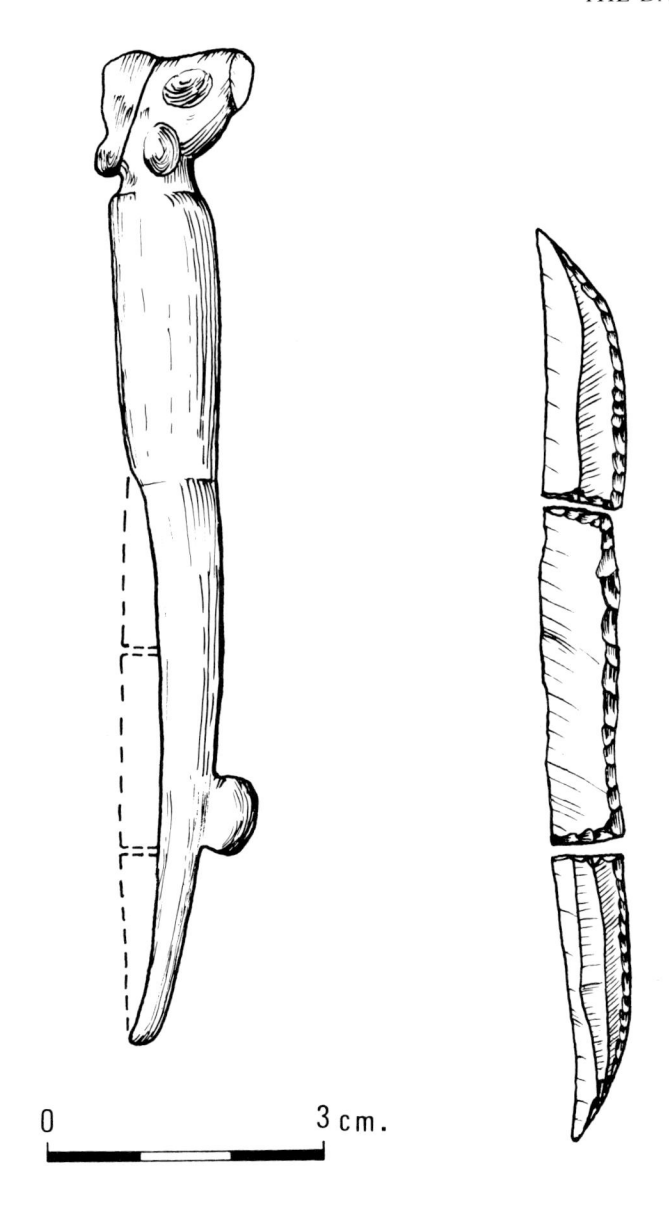

A sickle *(left)* and the flint blades used in it *(right)*

The Pursuit of Wealth

When people no longer wandered from place to place, hunting and gathering the wild foods they needed from day to day and week to week, material wealth took on a new importance. Suddenly, it was necessary to store up as much grain as possible, so that it would last the whole year. For this purpose, people began to build special structures called "granaries" in which to store their grain. It also became important to increase the production of other kinds of food. If the herds of sheep and goats could be increased, for example, then the supply of meat and milk would be large enough to provide for the population in case of hard times.

Land, too, suddenly became valuable in a way that it had never been valuable before. For hunters and gatherers, it was not the land itself but rather the wild game and vegetable foods it contained that had value. But when people learned how to grow their own foods, it no longer mattered what was to be found naturally on the land. If there was good soil and sufficient rainfall, the wild plants and animals could be cleared away and domesticated plants and animals could be raised there instead. Thus, for the first time, people began to own land and to consider it a form of wealth.

The Dawn of History

This new agricultural way of life gave rise to permanent towns and villages, where people lived all year round. Houses became larger and more complicated, since it was no longer necessary to move them about from time to time. Human beings began to make and keep a variety of things that would have been too heavy and bulky to carry about in the days of hunting and gathering. Heavy grinding equipment, clay jars and pots for storing and cooking, furniture, and many other items became commonplace. People had begun to acquire possessions; the old way of life was doomed.

As time passed, agricultural people became more and more numerous, taking more and more land, cutting down the forests, and driving the wild game farther and farther away from the places of human habitation. The numbers of hunting and gathering people gradually declined. Some hunters and gatherers converted to the new way of life, others moved away in search of better hunting grounds, and still others probably just died out. Slowly, agricultural society spread over the earth.

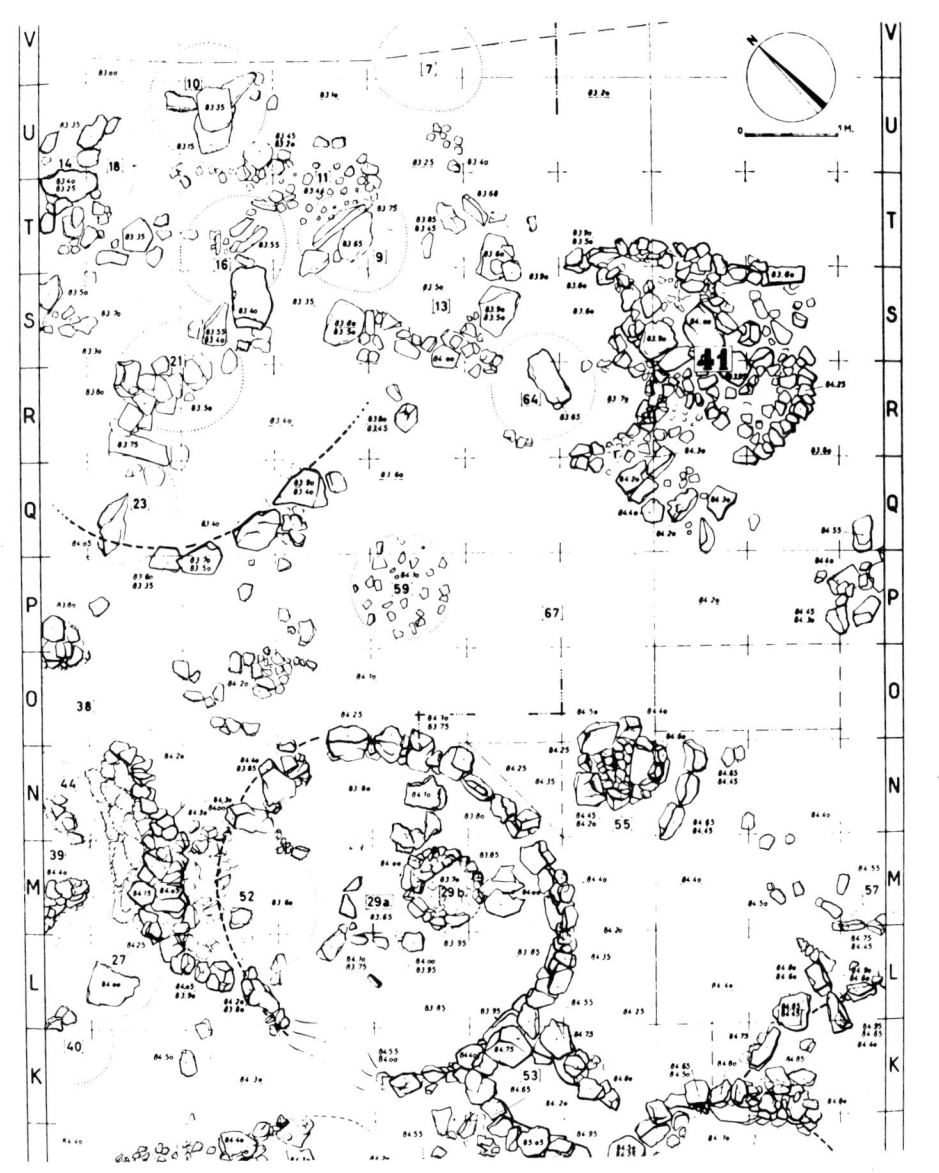

An archaeologist's drawing of circular structures discovered in the ruins of a 12,000-year-old village in Israel

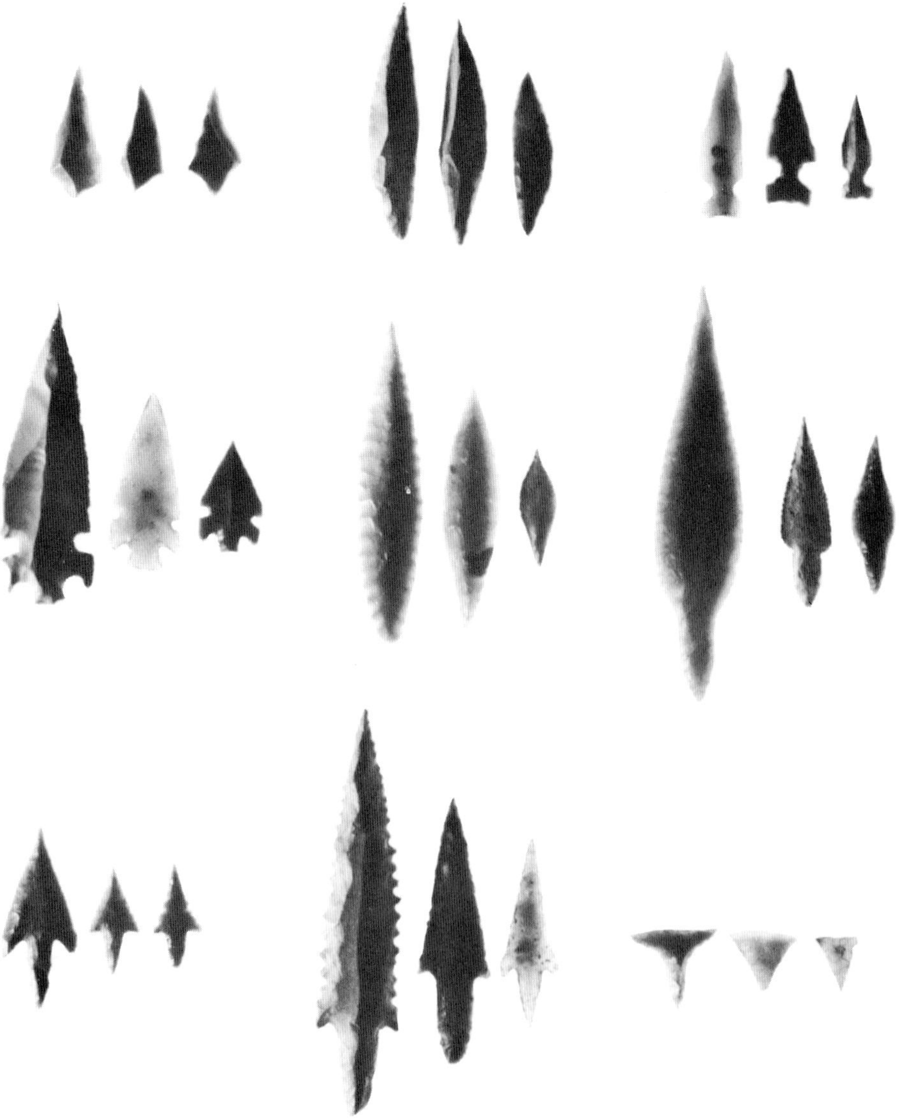

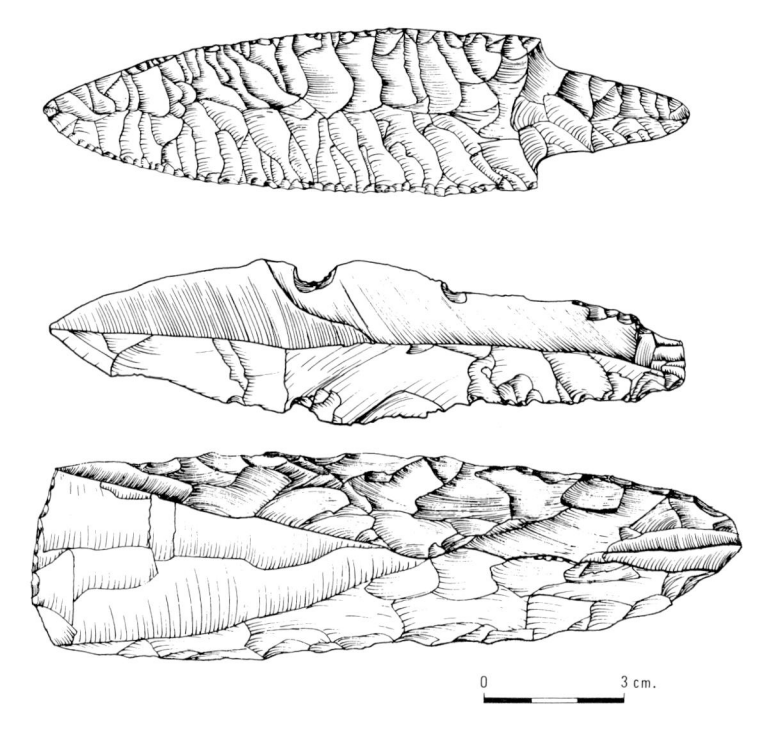

Typical tools from the end of the Stone Age, between 10,000 and 5,000 years ago. *Left:* Arrowheads of various types. *Above:* Top and center, knives; bottom, a celt.

At the same time, villages grew into towns and towns grew into cities. In the Mediterranean area, in the Far East, and in the Americas, civilizations gradually arose in or near the regions where agriculture first began. With the appearance of cities and of written records, prehistory ended and the age of history began. Looking back, we can see that the historical period has, in fact, only just started. It is, after all, only about 5,000 years old, a very short time in the total span of human life on earth.

At this very moment in history, the take-over by agricultural people that began in the days of our prehistoric ancestors is finally coming to completion. In the last 30 years, the few remaining hunting and gathering tribes have mostly either

This diagram shows the arrangement of houses in one area of the world's oldest city, Catal Hüyük in Turkey. The appearance of cities such as this marked the end of the prehistoric period.

died out or adopted an agricultural way of life. At this time there are only a few societies, hidden deep in the Amazon jungles and in the mountain valleys of remote Pacific islands, that are still living by hunting and gathering. In all likelihood, these last survivors too will disappear by the end of this century.

The human species has gone through many tremendous changes during the thousands of years that humans have lived on this planet. Now humanity faces a new crisis, brought about by pollution, overpopulation, and the destruction of natural resources. If we humans succeed in solving our current problems as successfully as our prehistoric ancestors succeeded in solving theirs, we have a long and exciting future ahead of us.

GLOSSARY

Acheulian A stone tool tradition developed by *Homo erectus*, in which handaxes were the most important items.

Australopithecus The first animal definitely know to be human. Australopithecus lived in East Africa between 3 million and 1 million years ago.

blades Long, thin flakes of stone, often with razor-sharp edges.

carbon-14 dating A method of dating ancient objects by measuring the amount of radioactive carbon that remains in a once-living material, such as wood, leather, or bone.

chopping tool A crude axe, often made of large pebbles and considered the first recognizable human tool.

cleaver A handaxe of the Acheulian tradition having a straight—instead of a pointed—cutting edge.

Cro-Magnons Fully modern *Homo sapiens* people, who appeared between 30,000 and 40,000 years ago.

culture A body of knowledge, including techniques of workmanship, handed down as a tradition through learning.

GLOSSARY

excavation — The process of digging up an archaeological site.

flake tool — A tool made from a flake, or chip, of stone.

handaxe — A large stone tool with a blunt or rounded end—which is held in the hand—and a sharp or pointed end—which is meant to be used as a cutting edge.

Homo erectus — The first human definitely known to have used fire. *Homo erectus* lived between roughly 1 million and 200,000 years ago.

Homo sapiens — The species of humans presently living, including both modern and Neanderthal types.

Oldowan — The pebble tool culture that started some 3 million years ago and ended between 1.5 million and 500,000 years ago, depending on the area.

potassium-argon dating — A method of dating certain volcanic rocks by measuring the amount of radioactive potassium they contain.

pressure flaking — A method of removing small flakes from stone tools by heating the tool and pressing against it with the point of a sharp instrument.

punch — A pointed instrument of bone or antler used for the precise removal of flakes.

Ramapithecus — An animal with teeth similar to human teeth that lived 15 or 20 million years ago. Ramapithecus may possibly be the ancestor of the human line of evolution.

site	A place where remains of ancient humans, or objects made by them, can be found.
spheroids	Large, rounded stones deliberately shaped as tools, appearing at the time of transition between Australopithecus and *Homo erectus*.
stratigraphy	A method of dating remains by determining which stratum, or layer, of a site they are associated with.
stratum	A layer of material deposited in a site by humans or wildlife that occupied it for a certain length of time.
Venus figurines	Small statuettes representing the female human body, with the sexual parts made in exaggerated size. These figurines are believed to have had magical significance in sex and fertility.

INDEX

Acheulian handaxe culture, 56, 59–60
agriculture, invention of, 83–84
art, 63, 73, 75
Australopithecus, 48, 53, 56, 60, 66
awl, 59, 78

baboons, 46
blade, 76
bone points, 79
brain, human, 44–45, 53; development of, 8, 43
burial of dead, 66

canine teeth, used as weapons, 46, 53
carbon-14 dating, 32, 37
caves, 12, 67
chimpanzees, 40–41, 44, 54
chopping tools, 49, 51, 52, 53, 56
cities, development of, 86–87
civilization, 7–8, 87
cleaver, 58, 59
clothing, 68
cooking food, 61
Cro-Magnons, 73, 75–77
culture, development of, 43, 59

Darwin, Charles, 39–40
dating prehistoric finds, 30–32, 37–38
domestication of animals, 77, 83

environment, changes in, 14–15
erect posture, development of, 42–43
excavation, 14–15, 18–19

fire, mastery of, 60–62
flake tools, 49, 52, 53, 68

Goodall, Jane, 41
graves, 66

handaxe, 56, 57, 59, 63, 64, 68
history: definition of, 7; extent of, 7–8
Homo erectus, 56, 59–60, 62, 63
Homo sapiens, 62, 63, 66, 68, 81
hunting, 53, 60, 68, 81

incest, avoidance of, among macaque monkeys, 42

language, 43–44, 54, 59

macaque monkey, 42
mapping prehistoric sites, 16, 17–19
microliths, 79
mortar and pestle, 83, 84

Neanderthals, 39, 40, 66–68, 73
notcher, 59

Oldowan tools, 48–49, 51, 53, 56

Olduvai Gorge, 48
overpopulation in prehistoric times, 81

pebble tools, 48–49
potassium 40, 32
potassium-argon dating, 37
pressure flaking, 76–77
punch, 75–76

radioactive carbon, 30, 32
Ramapithecus, 46–47

scraper, 59, 78
sickle, 85
site, prehistoric, 12, 14, 16, 18, 31
spheroids, 52, 53

stone tools: characteristics of, 49; earliest, 48; identification of, 49–51; methods of making, 49, 51, 53, 75–76; significance of, in studying prehistory, 10. *See also* specific types of tools
stratigraphy, 31–32
stratum, 31

tool-making by chimpanzees, 41

Venus figurines, 75, 76

wealth, importance of, in late prehistoric period, 86
writing, invention of, 8
written records, 7, 10, 87

ACKNOWLEDGMENTS

The illustrations are reproduced through the courtesy of Avraham Ronen P. 13; 20–27; 29. Gaussin and Bordes P. 16–19; 87. Department of Antiquities and Museums, State of Israel 28; 33; 84. David Harris P. 33; 84. Massada P. 34–36; 69–72. After van der Kloot P. 44. Irven Devore P. 47. Drawings by Avraham Ronen P. 49–52; 54; 57–58; 64; 73; 77–80; 85; 89. Bordes P. 65. Vandermeerch P. 66. Prähistorische Sammlungen, Ulm P. 74. A. Marshack P. 75. Bosinski P. 76. Friedman and Burian P. 88. Melaart P. 90.

AVRAHAM RONEN is chairman of Prehistoric Studies in the Department of Archaeology at Tel Aviv University, Israel. A native of Israel, Dr. Ronen studied archaeology and geography at the Hebrew University of Jerusalem. In 1960, he was granted a scholarship by the French government to continue his education at the University of Bordeaux. Three years later, he received a doctorate from that institution in recognition of his work in the field of prehistoric archaeology. Since that time, Dr. Ronen has conducted archaeological excavations at many prehistoric sites in Europe and the Middle East.

RICHARD L. CURRIER received his A.B. and Ph.D. degrees in anthropology from the University of California at Berkeley. He has done field work in Mexico and in Greece and has taught anthropology both at Berkeley and at the University of Minnesota. Dr. Currier now devotes full time to writing and research.